FINANCIAL HEALTH FOR YOUNG PEOPLE

EVERYTHING YOU NEED TO KNOW
ABOUT REAL WORLD FINANCE

———————

FERGAL WALSH

COPYRIGHT

Copyright © 2021 Fergal Walsh

All Rights Reserved. No part of this book may be reproduced in any form by any electronic or printed means, including information storage and retrieval systems, without permission in writing from the publisher. Researched and written by Fergal Walsh. The author did not receive any form of payment or benefits from any third parties to influence any of the content within the guide.

The aim of this guide is to promote financial health and mental wellbeing. Any personal opinions expressed are those of the author only. The content is intended as educational material.

This book contains some factual information, including figures relating to FCA regulations and HMRC rules that are correct and up to date to the best of the author's knowledge at the time of publishing. Although best efforts are made to ensure all information is accurate and up to date, occasionally unintended errors and misprints may occur. Any investment/ financial opinions expressed are those of the author and are in no way connected to any regulated financial organisation the author may be associated with at any time in the future.

The information in this book is not intended to replace financial advice. Conduct your own research and speak to a suitably qualified professional before making any important decisions. The information in the book does not constitute financial advice, investment or tax advice. If you require financial advice tailored to meet your individual circumstances, please contact a regulated adviser for a recommendation tailored to meet your exact needs. You will find information in the book as to how to seek out tailored financial advice from a trustworthy source.

Before making any tax decisions, please employ the services of a qualified accountant or tax adviser.

ISBN: 978-1-9168878-0-0 (Paperback Edition 2021/2022)

Edited by Dearbhaile Walsh
Cover design by Dave Duffy @davezutekh

CONTENTS

INTRODUCTION 1

    Why have I written this book? 4
    How do I become good with money? 4
    "I wish they had taught me all this in school!" 5
    Mental Health and Financial Wellbeing 7
    What's in this guide? 7
    Balance 8
    Getting What You Want 8

EARN 10

    Different Ways to Get Paid 13
    Tax Codes 17
    How do I know if I'm on an Emergency Tax Code? 18
    What do I do if I'm on an Emergency Tax Code? 18
    Understanding Your Payslip 18
    Gross Pay / Net Pay 19
    National Insurance 19
    How much do you repay towards student loan debt? 21
    Advantages and Disadvantages of Working for Yourself 25
    Going It Alone the Right Way 26
    Limited Companies 27
    Which one is most appropriate if I go self-employed? 28
    What is an asset? 34
    I don't have any money to purchase assets that will give me a second form of income... 35
    Do I have to pay tax on side hustle income? 37
    Transferable Skills 38
    Finding Your Dream Job by Accident 39

SPENDING AND BUDGETING 40

    Payday Millionaire Syndrome 40

Learn to Shop Around 42
Don't Be Overcharged for Essential Bills 42
Check your Direct Debits and Standing Orders 43
Watch Out for Recurring Payments 43
Watch out for Scams 44
The Importance of an Emergency Fund 45
Priority Payments 45
Priority Payments... With a Bit of Wiggle Room 46
Discretionary / Luxury spending 47
Making a Budget Plan 47
Using Budgeting Tools 48
Need help putting together a budget? 49
Saving by Default 50
What if you just can't hold on to your savings? 51
Multiple Savings Pots 52
Having More Than One Goal 54

SAVING VS INVESTING 55

Inflation 56
Interest 57
Saving vs Investing 58
Risk 59
What is Volatility? 60
Choosing a Savings Account 61
Why is it useful to have some investments that offer a higher return than a savings account? 63
Compounding Interest 63
Don't Pay Tax on your Savings 65
What are ISAs for? 66
ISA Allowances 67
Will taking money out affect my allowance? 67
What are the different types of ISAs? 67
What is the difference between each type of ISA? 68
What happens to my Junior ISA when I turn 18? 69
Taking Professional Advice 72

Innovative ISA big risks 74
Benefits of a Lifetime ISA 75
How does a LISA work? 76
What can I put in a Lifetime ISA? 76
LISA Risks 76
Can I transfer a LISA between different providers if I see one with a better rate? 77

INVESTING 78

Investing Can Seem Daunting 78
Important Notice about Investment 79
How are investment assets usually held? 80
What is Investment Risk? 80
What are the most common investment assets? What are the risks with each? 81
BUY TO LET INVESTMENTS 83
Why Owning Buy to Let Property isn't as Attractive as it Once Was 84
Bond Risks 86
What exactly is a "Share"? 86
What is the Stock Market? 86
Stock Market Returns 88
Stocks and Shares Risks 89
What to put in a Stocks and Shares ISA? 90
Active Funds 92
Active Fund Costs 92
Active Fund Risks 93
Passive Funds 93
Passive Fund Costs 94
Passive Fund Risks 94
Active vs Passive Investment Products 94
Popular Beginner Strategies for Long Term Investing 95
Understanding your Attitude to Investment Risk 97
What is Cryptocurrency? 99
Should I invest in Crypto? 100

Crypto Highs and Lows *101*
Crypto Scams *101*
What has caused this rise in fraud cases? *103*
What sort of scams are most common? *103*
What can I do to avoid being scammed? *104*
What do I do if I think I have been a victim of a scammer? ... *105*

BORROWING AND DEBT 106

What are the Most Common Types of Debt for Young People?
 .... *108*
How do young people get into problem debt? *109*
What is a Credit File? *110*
How Can I Check My Credit File? *111*
How Can I Improve My Credit File? *112*
Paying off your credit/store card *116*
Pay in Instalment Options – "Death by 1000 Cuts" *118*
Good Debt *120*
Bad Debt *121*
Payday Loans *122*
Debt to Pay for Everyday Items *123*

MENTAL HEALTH AND FINANCIAL WELLBEING 124

Dangers for "The Lost Generation" *125*
What are mental health issues and how do they affect young people? *126*
What is Depression? *127*
What is Anxiety? *129*
Coping with the pressure of financial goals *130*
Benefits to support you if you are struggling *130*
Making Smart Purchases *131*
Finding the Right Support *132*
Avoiding Con Artists *133*
Not Falling for the "Too Good to be True" *134*
COVID-19 and the Global Pandemic *135*
Effects of Social Media *136*

Targeted Advertising *137*
Gambling *138*
In-Game Purchases *138*
Don't Be So Hard on Yourself *140*
Practicing Mindfulness *140*
Personal Development *141*
Declaring Bankruptcy *142*
IVA *143*
Debt Charities: StepChange *144*
Who Else Can I Turn To? *145*
Mental Health and Money Toolkit *145*
The Bottom Line *146*

THE RISE OF CASUAL GAMBLING 147

From the High Street to Your Pocket *147*
The Law on Gambling *148*
Society's View on Gambling *148*
"The Bookie Always Wins" *149*
Gambling and Young People *150*
"Once the Fun Stops, Stop" *151*
How can I tell if I have a problem with gambling? *152*
What can I do if I think I might have a gambling problem? ... *153*
If you are worried about your gambling or the gambling of someone close to you, reach out. *153*
First Steps to Break the Habit *154*

PROPERTY: RENTING VS BUYING 156

Why it's important to think about home ownership early *157*
Pros and cons of renting and buying *158*
How do you get a good deal renting? *159*
What do I need to know about renting? *159*
Are all rental homes the same? *160*
What kind of rental agreements are there? *161*
Five tips for getting the best deal when you are renting: *162*
What Is A Lifetime ISA? *167*

What do I need to know before opening A Lifetime ISA if I plan to buy a house? *167*
How do I get a good deal buying? *168*
Why should I want to buy a house? *169*
What is a Mortgage? *170*
How much should I expect to pay for a mortgage? *170*
When can I get a mortgage? *172*
What Is "The Property Ladder" *174*
When do people usually buy their first homes? *175*
What is the average price for buying a home? *176*
What happens if I can't keep paying my mortgage? *176*
How can getting on the property ladder help my mental health? *177*
Living at home as a way to save *178*
Speak to a Mortgage Adviser *178*

KEEPING YOURSELF FINANCIALLY HEALTHY 180

Keep Yourself Educated *181*
Seek Professional Advice *181*
Take A Step Back Every So Often *182*
A Goal Without a Plan is Just a Wish *183*

FUTURE PLANNING..185

Emergency Planning *185*
How do I prepare for the unexpected? *186*
What are the chances? *186*
Bad things happen in life but if you are prepared for them, they won't seem so bad *187*
What if I get sick or critically ill? *188*
"Fail to Prepare, Prepare to Fail." *188*
Introducing Protection Products *189*
Car Insurance *189*
Insurance for Younger People *190*
Protection Example *190*
Let's have a look at the most common insurance products ...*191*

What are the benefits of getting protection in place early? ..192
Writing a Will 193
Pension Planning 194
What is a Pension?...194
Auto Enrolment 195
State Pension...195
Pensions – The Ticking Time Bomb...196
Start Early and Worry Less 197
When do I want to retire? 198
The Importance of Becoming Financially Literate 199
An Exciting Lifelong Journey Ahead..200
Suggested Further Reading / Viewing 201

FINAL THOUGHTS 204

Using Your Newly Discovered Knowledge 204
Make Learning A Habit...205

INTRODUCTION

My name is Fergal Walsh, and I'm a financial planner based in the North of England.

I started working for one of the biggest UK banks not long before the financial crash of 2008. You may have heard of this event being referred to as the "Credit Crunch", although I think that name makes it sound more like an Aldi own brand breakfast cereal as opposed to a worldwide economic disaster. Whatever you want to call it, it was the beginning of a rough time for many people, causing millions to lose jobs and homes.

The panic and knock-on effects were not unlike what we saw happen as a result of the Covid-19 pandemic that started in the first half of 2020.

In 2008, it was a failure of the banking systems that started in the US that went on to push all the biggest banks in the UK almost to the point of collapse.

In my first finance job aged 20, my role involved collecting money from customers who had not paid back the bank what they owed. Not a very glamorous job, but I didn't mind it because I was used to being sworn at.

(I'm originally from Derry in Ireland where verbally abusing each other is a national pastime).

Sitting at a desk with a phone in a huge open plan office with three floors I was surrounded by dozens of other staff who each spoke to up to 10 customers an hour chasing down money that was owed. This was my first glimpse behind the curtain, seeing first-hand the issues that were affecting people up and down the country.

My next job after that was helping people deal with their debt issues by offering support over a period of time and helping them get a better grip of their finances in order to get back on track. I did this for many years.

I am now in my mid 30s and I am a senior financial planner working for a large firm working out of a City Centre office that provides financial advice for people all over the UK. I have always liked talking to people from different backgrounds, learning about their lives and getting to know them.

When I spoke to people who had really struggled to manage their finances, I always tried to get inside their heads a little bit and understand how they ended up this way and tried to identify patterns / themes.

I have also come to notice strong trends and patterns of behaviour when dealing with clients who have amassed huge fortunes and are living very comfortable lives.

Every week, Monday through Saturday, I sit down with people and help them plan for the future and enable them to set achievable goals to enable them to live comfortable lives, whilst at the same time ensuring that their families will be okay if their circumstances change for the worse.

I have spoken to thousands of people who found themselves struggling with their financial health (this is something that can affect people from all walks of life.

It affects people who earn big salaries as well as those who struggle to find work).

"Why on Earth would the banks and credit card companies allow people to get into this sort of trouble?" you might ask. That is something we will explore in this book and look at how to avoid it ever happening to you.

Over the years a series of big scandals rocked the confidence of the general public. For example, you may remember hearing increasingly annoying and desperate ads on TV talking about how banks and finance companies made obscene amounts of money from Payment Protection Insurance on loans and credit cards; this was a money-making wheeze that left the general public out of pocket to the tune of billions of pounds. There was a lot of pressure applied to borrowers to take this product.

In fact, many people didn't need this insurance they were sold, or were unaware they were even paying for it in the first place!

When we consider examples like this, it is clear that there are people working high up in the finance industry who are happy to take advantage of members of the public who aren't clued up, and I feel it is fair to say that some of these companies do not have the wellbeing of the general public at heart.

Why have I written this book?

In all the different roles I have worked in, what has surprised me over the years was just how many people out there are very successful, work very hard and earn a lot of money, yet still go on to suffer dire consequences due to a lack of what is known as financial literacy.

Financial literacy is the possession of the set of skills and knowledge that allows an individual to make informed and effective decisions with all their financial resources.

I suppose to put it simply you could describe financial literacy as what you would describe as "being good with money". But what exactly does that mean?

How do I become good with money?

This led me to think back to my own education growing up. Sure, like everyone else, I learned about Pythagoras' Theorem and Trigonometry and just about scraped my way through my exams without too much anguish.

That being said, I still to this day have recurring anxiety dreams about arriving to class not having done my maths homework.

It is becoming harder and harder for young people to get on the property ladder, and pension plans are not as generous as they used to be. To add insult to injury, wages have not gone up in real terms since before the financial crash of 2008.

As a result, this generation will have to be much more proactive in saving and planning than their parents ever did. That's why reading up on books such as this one and becoming financially literate will be so important.

Therefore, I believe that it is essential to nurture and maintain financial health and wellbeing from as early as possible.

That's why I hear a lot of people my age saying the following:

"I wish they had taught me all this in school!"

I've undertaken extensive training on my journey towards becoming a financial planner and I am constantly reading and keeping track of changes in the markets which helps me understand some of the challenges we face.

The countless hours I have spent talking to ordinary people about their finances made me realise that the formal education that exists in schools today does not set people up to successfully navigate the challenges and obstacles they will encounter when they start out in the world of work.

When I talk to the young apprentices that join my firm today, it is very clear that not much has changed since I finished school 16 years ago.

If I had a quid for every time I've heard the words "I WISH THEY HAD TAUGHT ME ALL THIS IN SCHOOL" I would be able to retire today. (Actually, that's a massive exaggeration. I might have enough for a large Chinese takeaway or something, but nonetheless I have heard it more times than I care to count).

Amongst young people I speak to, and parents of young people I speak to, there is a general feeling that school does not equip you to deal with real world finance in the way that it should.

By no means am I slagging off schools or teachers here; I know they have very stressful jobs with shedloads of paperwork to keep on top of. Some of my close friends and family members are teachers. Trust me, I understand how stressful the job is.

Learning to be financially literate doesn't fit neatly into any one subject and requires quite a few different skills and a bit of life experience, so it is hard to nail this within the strict curriculum that is laid down.

There have been some very impressive attempts to promote financial literacy in schools in recent times led by money guru Martin Lewis, but some charities are still of the opinion that more needs to be done.

Mental Health and Financial Wellbeing

The effects of Covid-19 on young people cannot be ignored. Mental health problems at an all-time high, the job market becoming increasingly difficult to break into, and the economy looking somewhat uncertain for the foreseeable future, it seems that more than ever there is a need for more support for young adults getting ready to take on the world.

With this in mind, I thought it would be the perfect time to put together a handy guide, written in easy to understand English, free of any jargon, to help young people understand the challenges that they will face as they prepare themselves for adult life in the roaring 20s!

What's in this guide?

In this book I will spell out the main things you need to master in order to be financially literate.

I will discuss the stresses relating to money that exist in modern society and how to develop a positive attitude towards finance.

You will be able to use this guide to understand how to earn, spend wisely, save diligently, borrow sensibly, get on the property ladder, set goals and then how to maintain this financial health you have built up.

You should aim to enter into a healthy relationship with money as early as possible and this should make it easier for you to live a comfortable, prosperous life.

Balance

<u>Money is not everything.</u> It is however a very useful tool that allows you to have more options in life and if used correctly, it can be used to allow you more time to do things that you enjoy doing.

Getting What You Want

When it comes to getting what you want in life, firstly you must believe that you can get it, then set a plan with well-defined goals so you can do your best to make it a reality. If it comes unstuck, you simply dust yourself down and take a deep breath.

Where possible, learn from any mistakes or areas where you might do things better next time and then just keep right on going towards your goal.

Having well defined goals and a focused mindset, alongside a bit of knowledge that you will be able to take from this book, will set you well on your way towards financial health and success.

Chapter 1

EARN

For most people, in order to live a comfortable life, you must earn money.

We are fortunate to live in a country with a welfare system, meaning that if you cannot find work or you are too sick to work then there are various taxpayer funded benefits that will help you out.

However, if you are healthy and of working age, unless you are the heir to a huge family fortune you will most likely have to get up 5 or 6 days a week and go to work. The bills won't pay themselves.

WHEN NOT IN WORK

How do I get benefits when I'm not working?

If you are over 16 and are not in employment you may be entitled to benefits. There are many publicly funded benefits that can support you if you are looking for work like Job Seekers Allowance or Universal Credit.

There are also benefits you can get if you are sick, including both physical and mental disabilities.

You can speak to the Citizens Advice Bureau who have benefits experts who can help finding out what you are entitled to.

There is an awesome guide on the Mental Health and Money Advice website that covers everything you need to know about Universal Credit: what it is, whether you are eligible to get it and how to apply. It also has information on applying for Universal Credit if you have any mental health issues. The guide also explains how you can challenge a decision made by the Department of Work and Pensions if it doesn't go your way.

There is also a benefits calculator as well as other useful resources. Check it out here:

https://www.mentalhealthandmoneyadvice.org/en/welfare-benefits/universal-credit-mental-health-guide/introduction-to-universal-credit/

GETTING PAID

When it comes to making money, you can work for a company or work for yourself. Or both.

Most very wealthy people will have more than one income source.

They will have what is called **active income** (i.e. their main day job) and **passive income**.

For most young people starting out in the world of work you will be earning just active income.

Active income is the money you get in the form of salary, wages, tips, or commissions you get in exchange for the work you do. On the other hand, passive income is the money you earn by doing, well, not a lot to be honest.

"That sounds great!" I hear you say. "I chose the second one where you don't have to do anything."

Unfortunately, it's not quite as straightforward as that.

For many people, a long-term goal is to be able to use money that they earned by putting in hard work doing their day job to be able to use it to earn them passive income.

Have you ever dreamed of earning money while you sleep? Passive income is money that you can earn by renting out property that you own or reaping the rewards from investments that you have made.

You will undoubtedly come across YouTube videos explaining how you can get rich quick or make passive income by doing nothing.

Unfortunately, most of these videos are made by people who aim to trick you and get your money that you worked hard to earn so that they can make a lot of money overnight by acting dishonestly.

Of course, it is possible that you could buy a lottery ticket and match every number and become a millionaire overnight. I, myself, do not gamble but I understand some people like to believe that it could be them (I would rather keep the £2 and invest it but that's just me - I am a geek).

Just remember, according to the National Lottery website, the chances of hitting the jackpot and matching all numbers is one in 45,057,474.

It is a nice fantasy, however anyone online who tells you that you can make huge amounts of money in a matter of weeks, showing you their (rented) sports car and flashing wads of cash should not be given any of your precious time.

The cold hard reality is that there are no shortcuts, and you need to work hard and set goals in order to succeed.

Different Ways to Get Paid

The writer Mark Twain once said, "Find a job you love doing and you will never work a day in your life".

A nice sentiment but I don't know exactly how you would manage to instantly find the job you love on your first attempt without ever stacking shelves or doing some call centre work at some stage along the way!

Nit-picking aside, Mr Twain died leaving an estate of around $14,000,000 in today's money so I'm guessing he enjoyed his work.

Nevertheless, he was right. Finding a job that you enjoy doing makes a huge difference to your life.

When you hear your alarm clock going off each morning, if your body is paralysed with dread and horror in anticipation of the day that lies ahead, maybe you need to look for something different that you look forward to.

It can be a difficult balance because the skills you have that can earn the most money may not be the skills that you enjoy practicing.

If you can find something that pays quite well and offers a route for career progression while still allowing you to stay happy in your role then you are probably on the right path.

TAX

There is a corny old saying that says "Only two things are guaranteed in life: Death and taxes."

When you start earning money you will notice some deductions on your wage slip. There are lots of different forms of tax that the government imposes on people.

The main tax you will need to know about when you are starting out is **Income Tax.**

Tax is a deduction taken from citizens and businesses. It pays for things like:

The National Health Service	Government Functions
Free Primary and Secondary Education	Public Transport
Emergency Services	Waste and Environmental Services
Military Defence	Benefits
The Justice System (Courts etc)	Social Housing

There are various forms of tax payable in different scenarios but the main one that you absolutely need to understand is income tax.

The amount of tax you pay depends on how much money you earn.

Income Tax is chargeable on basically all forms of income, i.e. wages and salary from working for a company, your profits if you run a business etc.

However, you don't usually pay Income Tax on all your taxable income. This is because most people qualify for one or more **allowances**. An allowance is an amount of otherwise taxable income that you can have tax-free each tax year. This year runs from April to April and these rules get updated each year.

For most people, you can earn up to £12,570 each year before you start paying tax. It's known as your **personal allowance.**

One of the most common misunderstandings is that the tax rate is applied to the entire annual earnings, but it is actually applied in tiers or stages. So, keep in mind the first £12,570 you earn, you pay nothing. Then, on earnings in the next bracket up you pay 20%, and so on.

What's important to remember is it's only the portion of your earnings that falls into the bracket you'll pay a different rate on – the first £12,570 is untouched, anything above £12,570 up to £50,270 is taxed at 20%, etc. The table below shows the current tax rules in the UK – There are different rules in Scotland so you can check online to see the most up to date rules for you.

https://www.moneyadviceservice.org.uk/en/articles/scottish-income-tax-and-national-insurance

Rate	2021/2022
0%	If you earn between £0 to £12,570 annually, you don't have to pay any income tax. This is your "personal allowance".
Basic rate 20%	On earnings between £12,571 to £50,270 each tax year, you pay 20% of what you earn to Her Majesty's Revenue and Customs on this portion of your income. *But* this is not applied to the first £12,570.
Higher rate 40%	£50,271 to £150,000. On these earnings you will pay 40%.*
Additional Rate 45%	Once you earn over £150,000 any earnings in this bracket are charged at 45%.

*Once you earn over £100,000 a year, your "personal allowance" of £12,500 starts to reduce bit by bit. Once you earn £125,000 the £12,500 allowance is removed completely.

Example of how Income Tax is applied

Brendan lives in London and earns £55,000 a year as an employee of a software company.

He will pay nothing on his income up to £12,570. On his income between £12,571 and £50,270, he'll pay income tax at 20% - known as the basic rate. The portion that falls into the higher bracket, i.e. on everything over £50,271 he will pay income tax at 40%.

Tax Codes

Everyone has a tax code which reflects how much tax you pay. This will be found on your wage slip.

An emergency tax code is used if HMRC (the tax office) does not have enough information about you to send your employer the correct code. This might happen if you start your first job and get your first wages part of the way into the financial year.

It could also be applied if you start getting a secondary form of income on top of your main wage.

This will mean that you pay tax on all of your income and you will not be able to get access to the usual personal allowance of £12,570 on which you pay 0% tax.

How do I know if I'm on an Emergency Tax Code?

Your wage slip will show your tax code. If you're on an emergency tax code your payslip will show one of the following codes: **1250 W1, 1250 M1 or 1250 X.**

What do I do if I'm on an Emergency Tax Code?

You should speak to your employer and should be able to correct this. If they can't sort it or you are self-employed, you can contact HMRC to find out what you need to do to correct it and reclaim the tax you've overpaid.

As we will look at later, if you are self-employed, it is worth speaking to a reputable accountant.

Understanding Your Payslip

Everyone who is employed is entitled to an individual payslip (either printed out or online) at the time they are paid. It is important to understand how your pay is worked out. If you are employed and therefore paid via PAYE (Pay as you Earn), your payslip contains important information like your gross and net pay and your tax code.

Make sure you check this regularly to make sure you are being paid correctly.

Do not be afraid to query anything you do not understand or that you feel is wrong on your payslip.

Gross Pay / Net Pay

Your **gross pay** is the total amount before deductions like tax, national insurance and pensions etc.

If a recruiter tells you "this job pays £30,000 a year", they are referring to the gross pay.

Your **net pay** is what you have left after the deductions (tax, national insurance and pension) have been taken off.

This gross/net difference can be confusing. The way I remember which one is which, is by using this silly method: the gross figure will be fatter and when I eat lots of fatty food, I feel gross. Net is how much you end up with "in the net" after deductions.

National Insurance

National Insurance contributions are a tax on earnings, which are paid by employees and employers and help to build your entitlement to certain state benefits that will be useful later on in life, such as the State Pension and Maternity Allowance. For example, If you haven't built up enough during your working life, you might not get the full state pension when you stop working in old age.

If you are self-employed, always consult an accountant to make sure you are paying the correct level of national insurance contributions.

GETTING THE JOB YOU WANT

To secure the job of your dreams you will most likely need to learn about your craft and undergo some training and learning. There are a few ways that you can go about getting this training.

UNIVERSITY

Traditionally, the way into more sought-after professions, the route to go down was through University courses. However, in the last decade, student fees have increased significantly.

Student Finance is available to pay for these courses and once in work, you will be expected to pay this back and pay some interest on this (a charge to the company for providing the service).

Therefore, it is now more important than ever to ensure that you do research into the course you plan to do and understand how useful this will be to you in your career. You should also establish how much this will cost and what implications this student debt will have on you later in life.

Student Finance in the UK is provided by the Student Loan Company. According to research published in September 2020 by Statista, students graduating from English universities in the year 2020 will have incurred an average of £ 40,2800 of student loan debt, compared with £24,9600 pounds in Wales, £23,5200 pounds in Northern Ireland, and £13,8900 in Scotland.

Some wealthy families might have the ability to help their kids with the costs of a university education, however many students will have needed to borrow more than the figures quoted above to cover additional costs that may be treated differently from the money lent out by the Student Loan Company.

How much do you repay towards student loan debt?

How much you repay depends on how much you earn.

You start paying once you go over a threshold for your weekly or monthly income. You repay 9% of the amount you earn over £2,214 a month (before tax and other deductions). You do not pay anything back while your income is under that threshold, but interest is added on from when you get your first payment.

Therefore, if you are not earning enough to pay anything towards the repayment the interest will continue to be tacked on over time.

Example of student loan repayment

Gemma is paid weekly, and her income changes each week. This week her income was £600, so it is over the weekly threshold of £511. Her income was £89 over the threshold (£600 minus £511). She will pay back £8 (9% of £89) this week.

This might not seem much but if you start to earn more this can really make a noticeable difference, especially if you get paid more some months than others e.g. if you get one large annual bonus or a lot of your income is paid via quarterly commission payments.

Student loan payments are still classified as debt, but it is important to know that student loan debt is not treated the same way as other forms of money you owe, being seen as "good debt" as it is an investment in your future prospects.

If you do not earn enough to have to pay student loan repayments and this is the case for most of your career, eventually the loan will be written off and this will not have negative consequences on you. We will look at debt in more detail in the Borrowing chapter.

APPRENTICESHIP SCHEMES

In 2009 The United Kingdom government introduced a scheme called Apprenticeships in England, Wales and Northern Ireland.

If you know what you want to do, these schemes can be an excellent way of getting into work earlier than people who go to university. These schemes are open to people between the ages of 16 and 24. They offer the benefits of being able to work alongside experienced professionals, gaining some real-life work experience whilst also working towards a nationally certified qualification. The other main advantage over a university course is that there is no need to build up any student debt.

On an apprenticeship scheme, the pay will be much lower than you would expect if you were doing the job on a permanent contract. Many apprentices are paid £4.15 an hour, although you may qualify for reductions in the cost of some bills and transport costs.

It is worth trying to check out online forums and speak to anyone you know who has done a particular apprenticeship to try and understand if it is the right option for you.

You will want to ensure you are going to be spending your time well as there will potentially be a lot of work being done for very little pay. It also makes sense to ensure it is done with a view to getting you into a job in an industry you intend to work in otherwise it could be a waste of your time.

You can learn more about apprenticeship schemes at https://www.apprenticeships.gov.uk/

If you do not know what you want to do immediately after leaving school or college, maybe work doing something you enjoy while you make up your mind. Wait before paying for an expensive degree.

Keep in mind that it may take you a while for you to work out what you are interested in. It is worth knowing that there are often a range of professional qualifications that you can do at any point alongside your work, and these can help you get a job in your chosen field. If the course or qualification relates to something that you do, the government will sometimes allow you to claim the cost of these back by allowing you to pay less tax the following year.

SELF-EMPLOYMENT

Some people like the idea of being their own boss. Most people who work for themselves will start as a sole trader and then they may go on to form a limited company as their business grows so that they can access government grants, claim back expenses and legally reduce their tax bill. Most of the most famous and successful business figures will have owned their own companies rather than work for someone else.

It is often the case that people work for someone else while they learn their trade and build up some money to be comfortable before going out on their own.

The advantage is that even if you aren't very good at your job yet, you will still have a contract that will guarantee you some basic income and benefits while you get better or find the job that is exactly right for you! If you were self-employed and not good at what you do, you might not get paid anything at all.

Advantages and Disadvantages of Working for Yourself

There definitely are perks:

- You get to be in charge of your own time and not being told how or when to do things.
- You control how much to charge for your products or services.
- You might be able to keep more of the money that is generated than you might if you worked for someone else.
- You don't have to negotiate for a better salary, you could just work harder or price your service/ product difficulty.

There are also disadvantages:

- Having no basic wage to rely on so it could be more difficult to plan for future financial goals.

- You won't get paid for sick days and for some people, not being told to arrive at 8am will mean that work doesn't start until 1pm so not much money gets made. Unless you are very focused and consistent, self-employment might not be for you.
- Starting from scratch can be difficult if you have no money for marketing or to buy equipment depending on what you plan to do.

Going It Alone the Right Way

If you choose to take this step, ensure that you've thought about it carefully. Make sure you don't get any nasty surprises if you do choose to go it alone. If you choose to set up as self-employed you will probably start out as what is called a "sole trader".

Speak to someone who does something similar (if it is a friend this is ideal but be aware that you could be setting yourself up as their competition). If you do not know anyone doing what you plan to do and you are okay being a bit cheeky, why not contact them posing as a prospective client and ask them some questions to get a better understanding as to how they work.

It's very important you speak to an accountant before you start working so that you can get things set up the right way and you understand what is required of you so that you don't have any nasty surprises later on.

You can get into good habits of putting aside a portion of your earnings for tax and national insurance.

If you're working as a sole trader, you need to:

- Tell Her Majesty's Revenue and Customs (the tax man) so that you can make sure you are paying the right amount of tax and national insurance contributions.
- Set up a business bank account.
- Keep track of your sales (profits / losses) and expenses. This helps you keep track of how your company is doing and helps you with invoicing. You can get apps like QuickBooks that can make this easier for you. It will be required when it comes time to pay your tax.

Limited Companies

If you start earning well working for yourself, you may want to start your own limited company.

Setting up a limited liability company is a way of establishing a separation between the business owner (you and any partners you chose to work with) and the company you own. This means that you can keep your own personal finances separate from that of the business.

A limited company can get more favourable rates of tax and government grants. For example, it means that in some circumstances, if your business falls behind on debts or the company gets sued, you can protect your own assets (things you own).

If you couldn't pay a debt for example, only items owned by the business could be seized, whereas if you were a sole trader your own assets would be at risk because there is no separation between you and your business.

This route is not as straightforward as being a sole trader. It comes with more responsibilities and keeping on top of these can be time consuming and expensive. You must set a director and secretary and keep up with a lot of paperwork and regularly publish public information about your company.

- You must be over 16
- You have to register your company with Companies House
- Your company must keep up to date with required paperwork and publish public information annually
- If you do not take your responsibilities as a company director seriously, this can have very serious consequences for you personally.

This is by no means a watertight list of requirements. More information can be found here:
https://www.gov.uk/set-up-limited-company

Which one is most appropriate if I choose to go self-employed?

This is worth researching and weighing up carefully before you make a decision on this question.

It very much depends on what you plan to do and your plans for the future. Read the information on the government website listed above for further information if it is something you are considering.

The amount of business you expect to do will be an important factor. If you are just starting out it's likely working as a sole trader might be most appropriate, but it is worth talking through with an accountant if you think you are ready to set up a company.

FUTURE PROOFING YOUR JOB – THE RISE OF THE ROBOTS

The rise in artificial intelligence and computer automation is leading to a decline in jobs that were traditionally lucrative. Factory jobs have been in decline for many years. Car factories now have more robots than human employees.

There has been a huge amount of money invested in research into finding solutions that reduce the need for human input. The biggest cost for many businesses is staff. Take away wages, insurances, pensions, employee benefits etc, and the companies can make a lot more money as there's less being spent on human resources.

A recent piece of research carried out by Statista shows that over a million jobs in the UK are at risk due to the rise of driverless cars.

All those additional people out of work will make the jobs that are available much more sought after, meaning the job market is even more difficult to break into. A good question to ask yourself when you are starting to think about your future career would be "could this job be done by a computer in 5 or 10 years from now."

Around 1.5 million jobs in England are at high risk of some of their duties and tasks being automated in the future, Office for National Statistics (ONS) analysis shows. Automation may go on to claim as many as 47% of current jobs, according to a recent Oxford University study.

If you're planning a career path you may want to consider rethinking if your chosen career is among the following examples:

1 - Driver (Taxi / HGV)
2 - Bank Cashier
3 - Supermarket checkout assistant
4 - Receptionist / PA
5 - Postal worker
6 - Travel Agent
7 - Factory worker
8- Surgeon
9 - Soldier
10 – Telemarketer

Here is an example of 10 jobs that will be less affected by the rise of automation:

1 - Software developer
2 - Writer
3 - Human Resource Manager
4 - Graphic Designer
5 - Event Planner
6 - Solicitor
7 - Clergymen
8 - Dancer
9 - Social Worker
10 - Psychiatrist

You can see there appears to be a trend towards jobs that require more creativity and need good skills in interacting with other humans and understanding and conveying complex emotions; something that computers are unlikely to be able to do.

University isn't for everyone, especially considering the cost of student loans. If you have a career path that you know you want to follow, why go to university when free training can get you into the same position?

Obviously "vocational" employment such as law, medicine and dentistry which will hopefully land you a much higher paying role in the end and will always require a university degree, therefore the student loan will be paid back with the larger salary you would earn. Remember that if you do a degree course then do not complete it, the loan is still payable regardless of when you leave.

Seeking affordable training like an apprenticeship scheme or a foundation degree can be better for some. They can get you on the job market much earlier than traditional degrees. They also tend to teach more "real life skills", meaning your training makes you better at your job.

This means that you could be 21 with six years industry experience under your belt and no student debt.

Depending on the role you want to do, this can put you in a much better position to start climbing the job ladder.

Additionally, many **occupational qualifications** are much less expensive than an undergraduate degree. For example, a qualification in giving mortgage advice.

As long as it is from a list of recognised institutes of learning, the cost can often be paid for then claimed back through government incentives – they will change your tax code the following year to reimburse you for upskilling yourself. It's worth checking beforehand to see if you qualify.

HAVING MULTIPLE INCOME STREAMS

I think given the choice, most people would like to be wealthy - having a lot of money and not having to go to work seven days a week. But becoming "wealthy" isn't something that happens overnight.

Most people considered to be wealthy will have one thing in common: they will have money coming in from more than one place. We have talked about the idea of active and passive income. Active income is earned doing what we would consider traditional "work", such as working in a shop or fixing cars in a garage. Passive income is money that you make without doing any additional graft. Often this is earned from taking money you earned doing traditional work and then investing it into something that will continue to give you an income without having to do any additional work.

In today's digital world there are many other ways it can be obtained. For example, if you made a few YouTube videos that gave you a monthly income from advertising revenue, this ongoing income you receive could be described as passive (as people could continue to watch them and you don't have to keep doing the initial work over and over to get paid).

In a very famous book called "Rich Dad Poor Dad" by an author called Robert Kiyosaki, the author talks about how he learned how to become wealthy by learning about finance from a successful man who was the father of his friend Mike. His own dad had a good job but always seemed to be skint due to the outgoings he had each month. His dad advised him to follow the traditional route, work hard and get a job and this will lead to success.

Unconvinced by this, in a rather cruel move (in my humble opinion) he started to refer to Mike's dad as his "rich dad" and the lessons he learned changed the way he thought about money. For example, Robert takes the view that a home you live in is not an "asset" as it doesn't provide any income, it just creates more bills to pay and reduces cash flow. Obviously, a house does have value, but his theories all revolve around **cash flow** (i.e., how much money is actually going in and out of your pocket every month).

What is an asset?

Traditionally an asset would be deemed to be any item that is perceived to be of value. His point of view is that an asset that doesn't produce an income is a liability. i.e. something that makes you poorer day to day. He says liabilities take money out of your pocket and true assets should put money into your pocket and increase your cash flow and the amount of money you have to spend.

In summary, the book "Rich Dad, Poor Dad" explains how wealthy people take money earned from their day job, use this to purchase "assets" that generate income, and aim to have a number of methods in which they get paid.

He took the view that focusing all his energy into doing just one job that provided all his income was actually a riskier strategy than having a number of income streams. The reasoning being that if he was to lose his job, he would not be able to pay for all the liabilities he has due to the fact he doesn't have any other way of earning money.

This is a very simplistic way to look at things and I'm not saying I necessarily agree with all of his logic, however I like to mention it because this does bring up some interesting ideas that do make sense.

It's good to get into the mindset that you ideally want to end up with at least two or three forms of income. You want to use some of the money you earn doing your job to eventually invest in other assets that will let your money work for you rather than the other way around.

I don't have any money to purchase assets that will give me a second form of income... How do I achieve more than one income stream now?

Early on in life you are unlikely to have such a surplus of income to allow you to invest heavily right away. We will look at goals and budgeting in more detail a little later on.

In the meantime, how can you generate extra income? Start with what you are good at.

What was your favourite subject in school? If you can find something that you were better than average at (or great at) you can use this talent and put it to work for you.

Did you excel at coding? Did you enjoy creative writing? Do you like doing artwork or making music?

You can harness these skills and gain experience and some extra money by bidding for jobs on work freelancing sites like Fiverr.com or upwork.com.

Busy professionals may need a bit of graphic design work done but lack the skills. They might need a short story for a magazine on a deadline.

If you think you can handle this type of work, and you have the time, you can quickly build up a back catalogue of projects you have completed. Depending on how sought after your particular skill is, you can earn decent money for doing something that you enjoy.

SIDE HUSTLES

There are loads of little ways you can turn hobbies into money making side hustles.

Have you an eye for fashion or memorabilia? eBay can be a way of using your knowledge of a particular market to make some extra income.

For example, if you like trainers and you know there is a release for a limited-edition pair of trainers at 8am on a Friday, most people will not have the time or the inclination to queue up to buy them.

If you are not working that day, why not queue up and buy yourself a couple of pairs in a popular size then put them on an online marketplace like eBay?

The time taken queuing up for half an hour then listing and posting the trainers could earn you up to 30% of the cost of the items.

That could end up making you more than a day's wages by taking advantage of your knowledge of the marketplace and being a bit cheeky.

If the digital world is not for you, you can go for things like cutting neighbours grass / trimming their trees. If you are good with children, looking after the kids of family friends.

Do I have to pay tax on side hustle income?

Money earned as income as part of a side hustle will count towards your total taxable income. Keep in mind that the first £12,570 is non-taxable so if the total falls below that figure you do not pay tax on your income.

You may also qualify for a £1000 trading allowance on the first £1000 of self-employed income, but if you are unsure you can ring Her Majesty's Revenue and Customs (HMRC) and ask to make sure you stay on the right side of the tax man!

Further information is available on the government website: https://www.gov.uk/income-tax-rates

You will need to record money earned by using a self-assessment form to declare the income to the taxman (HMRC) in case your side hustle really starts taking off and starts becoming difficult for you to track, although this is what we call a good problem to have.

If your side project turns into a small business that is generating a healthy income, there is accounting software you can use to help you, for example QuickBooks, and you may also want to contact an accountant for help.

Transferable Skills

The great thing about expanding your skillset and gaining experience doing different things is that a lot of the skills you learn will probably come in handy in other projects you do in your career.

Did you have to negotiate a price for a piece of gardening work you proposed to do?

That will help you if you get a sales job. Did you have to learn some Photoshop skills when you printed T Shirts as a side hustle?

This could help you in all sorts of ways in various creative roles.

Finding Your Dream Job by Accident

You could even find your true passion by trying out different side hustles... It might be the case that the enjoyment you get drives you on and the money you make from your secondary income source starts to surpass the money you get from your main job that you find boring and you can pack it in entirely and then your life could be much more enjoyable as a result, doing what you love for a living.

Chapter 2

SPENDING AND BUDGETING

SPENDING SMART

Once you start getting paid, you will get that satisfying feeling of being able to look at your bank balance and see all that hard-earned dosh you worked for looking back at you.

Some people find this intoxicating and give in to the temptation of becoming a "weekend millionaire".

Payday Millionaire Syndrome

New Nike trainers for £180 and trips to Five Guys on payday weekend, then beans on toast every night until you get paid next month?

It's a very real temptation and the gratification you get spending that money can be addictive.

But when you start being disciplined and delaying that gratification the rewards you get in the long run are infinitely more satisfying.

Getting into good habits early will set you up nicely.

When you practice delaying that gratification it will mean that you can do amazing things that you would never have got to experience had you spent all your money in a frenzy just because it was there to be spent.

Can you resist buying those trainers you don't really need, or going on that night out on a Tuesday that will probably be expensive and pretty forgettable?

What if resisting that urge means that you can go on an unforgettable foreign holiday in the summer, or buy your first car when all your friends are still queuing in the rain waiting for the bus?

Now, of course I'm not saying you should walk around wearing a potato sack with arm holes cut in it with Tesco bags tied around your feet, or that you should stop going out to see your friends.

Everyone deserves a treat now and again and enjoying yourself is what life is about but if you can be a little bit disciplined and act sensibly when it comes to spending, it can get you into habits that will make things easier for you as you get used to budgeting for future goals.

Learn to Shop Around

Thanks to people like Martin Lewis and his campaigns, online content and TV programs, people are starting to get wise to the fact that big companies will charge whatever they can get away with to maximise profit.

Don't Be Overcharged for Essential Bills

Regulations have been brought in that makes it a requirement for energy companies to tell you if you are not on their cheapest tariff.

Be careful, it is important to be aware that they are not required to move you onto this tariff, they just have to tell you.

All those emails and letters that come through may appear to be junk, but they will have this info about the savings you could make in there somewhere.

Ultimately though it's on you to act.

The difference can be hundreds of pounds a year.

Some companies like Look After My Bills will do this for you for free (in return for a bit of commission from the providers).

It's worth regularly checking you aren't being fleeced because a lot of these huge mobile phone / energy / internet / satellite TV providers are notorious for charging as much as they can get away with to maximise profit for their shareholders.

Check your Direct Debits and Standing Orders

Most people choose to pay by direct debit as a handy method of keeping on top of your bills.

It's worth checking from time to time to make sure that you aren't paying for anything that you no longer use (gym membership, premium for old products, or services you aren't using any more).

Watch Out for Recurring Payments

A lot of apps on your phone now get paid via Apple store or Google Play Store.

This can make it difficult to keep track of exactly what you are paying for as the name of the service will not always show up on your statement.

Check with Google / Apple directly to see what exactly you are being billed for and cancel anything you don't use.

Continuous card transactions are often very similar and difficult to keep track of.

If you have some of these set up that you didn't request or authorise, you can cancel the payments by contacting your bank.

Just be careful that you don't cancel anything that you have signed a credit agreement for without checking with the company first, otherwise it could affect you negatively.

We will cover credit files in the Borrowing chapter.

Watch out for Scams

I have covered some of the most common scams to watch out for in the Avoiding Scams chapter.

BUDGETING

How to Budget

When it comes to managing your money effectively it's important to have a set budget you try to stick to each week or each month depending on how often you get paid.

If you are working for yourself it can be wise to look at your monthly bills and try to work out an average of your earnings so that you can afford monthly direct debits, otherwise this can become a headache.

The Importance of an Emergency Fund

This is one of the most important paragraphs in this book.

In financial advice we talk to all of our clients about the importance of having an emergency fund. This is a pot of money that you have easy access to that you can get your hands on in case of an unforeseen event.

The stock piece of advice is that 3 to 6 months' worth of earned income is the ideal amount to aim to have at your disposal.

Not many people have this. This can be especially difficult for someone starting out with limited excess income with a couple of goals they are working towards, but I feel it is always worth keeping in mind as a medium-term goal.

Any unexpected windfalls of cash that come your way could be held aside in this way to help protect you.

Priority Payments

There are certain payments that must be paid.

Examples of these are Rent / Mortgage / Council Tax / Utility Bills / Food / Car Insurance / Car Tax.

Some of these payments are non-negotiable. Rent and Council tax bills are usually set in stone.

It is however worth checking with your local council if you qualify for any reductions in council tax due to your circumstances (for example if you are a student or a single occupier in a property).

Utility bills like gas, electric and broadband have to be paid but it is very much worth your while shopping around for the best deal. There are many price comparison sites set up to help you with this.

Aim to do this at least once a year, as some of these companies can be quite crafty in enticing you in with an introductory rate then increases will creep in that you might not notice straight away.

Priority Payments... With a Bit of Wiggle Room

This is the part of your essential budget where you have a bit of discretion over your level of spending. Everyone needs to eat however take food shopping for example - buying just enough food for a meal or two each day in the local Sainsburys and then ordering a Deliveroo or an Uber Eats takeaway when there's nothing in can mean that your food bills spiral away out of control.

Buying in bulk in cheaper supermarkets like Aldi or Lidl once a week and having a store of canned goods and frozen vegetables to cover the majority of your meals, as well as getting into good habits such as batch cooking at the weekend, will massively decrease your food bill.

Discretionary / Luxury spending

This includes things like meals out, cinema tickets, socialising, designer clothes etc. This is down to your own personal preference, but it is worth always consulting your budget before you make any decisions to make purchases that fall in this category.

The author Terry Pratchett once said, "The reason that the rich were so rich, was because they managed to spend less money."

For example, spending a little more on good quality boots would mean they last for many years, whereas spending less on a pair of boots that are of lower quality will mean that they get worn out and let water in much quicker.

As a result, someone who buys a lower quality pair will have to buy again and again while the rich man will only have had to buy one pair.

The idea here is that by budgeting your money and investing in quality items you will have to replace them less often rather than regularly shelling out for more disposable items that fall apart easily.

Making a Budget Plan

One of the classic examples of a budget plan might be like this:

Priority Payments: 50%

Discretionary/ Luxury payments: 30%

Savings: 20%

Using example figures based on a budget of £2000 a month, that's £1000 on your housing, bills etc, £300 on lifestyle purchases. The remaining £200 can be used for saving towards goals.

This will not suit everyone – it may need to change depending on how much you earn because a lot of the priority payments such as rent or travel expenses aren't going to change depending on how much you earn.

Other people might say saving 20% of their income is too much to save, whereas some people who are laser focused on their goals might reduce the discretionary payments right down to increase the amount they can put in savings and put towards long term goals.

Using Budgeting Tools

There's an array of tools you can now use to keep track of your spending.

Some people keep track of their spending on Excel, but this is a bit too time consuming for me however if you are that way inclined it can be a great way to keep yourself in check.

Innovative new companies like Monzo and Revolut will allow you to set up your main current account with them and track your spending.

It can give you a regular breakdown as to where your money actually goes, using categories for example: Shopping, Eating Out, Transport, Entertainment.

This enables you to regularly check up on these to see where you are overspending and where you can try and make cutbacks. These tools will also allow you to set up savings pots and will help you save towards longer term goals.

Setting a budget allows you to be more mindful as to where your money goes.

It will encourage you to make better conscious decisions about what you spend your money on and see where you are overspending.

How often do you pop into your local coffee shop?

Could you cut out some of these visits by making a coffee at home? You really would be surprised by how quickly little amendments to your spending help you keep your outgoings under control.

Need help putting together a budget?

There are some amazing resources available on *The Money Charity's* Website.

The Money Charity are an awesome organisation who I turn to all the time in my role as a financial adviser as they publish up-to-date statistics about what's going on in terms of finance in the UK and they have tons of resources for young people getting to grips with finance.

They also have a great budget builder tool on their website.

They even have an app you can download for Android or iPhone.

The Budget Builder is a free to use interactive tool which allows you to create a customised budget that helps you track day to day spending.

You can set up a system that allows you to keep track of your money management on a daily basis and access it on different devices to stay completely on track. You can download it here for free:

https://budgetbuilder.themoneycharity.org.uk/

Saving by Default

This is a habit that if you get into it early on, you will never be short of a few quid.

"You can't spend it if it's not there"

Some people operate a system whereby their money goes into their account each month, and whatever is leftover at the end of the month, they will put that amount into a savings account. However, this isn't the most effective way to save money.

A much more effective method of saving is by setting up a savings pot whereby you work out your budget and establish how much you can afford to save.

Then at the start of each pay cycle, you automatically transfer a set amount into your savings so that you never see it in the first place.

This way you won't get tempted later in the month to overspend on luxury spending as it won't be available in your account.

What if you just can't hold on to your savings?

Some people find it very difficult to save.

Once you have worked out your budget and set your goals, having built up an emergency fund, you may get tempted to use your long-term savings to spend on things other than their intended purpose.

When I was in my 20's I thought I could outsmart myself by transferring the money into a secondary savings account then go back in and steal that money from myself. Ingenious, eh?

Eventually I had to come up with a more watertight method.

If you are the type of person who is easily tempted to go on nights out because of the fear of missing out (FOMO) or you find the money burning a hole in your pocket, then maybe you can do what I did when I was saving for my first property.

You can set up the savings account - set up an ISA or investment and keep it separate from your main accounts, in a separate bank or platform for example, so that you cannot easily just drag and drop funds into your main account.

If this isn't enough of a mental barrier for you, enlist the help of an older, more sensible family member who you trust and ask them to open an account on your behalf where you can transfer the money.

This third party must be under strict instruction not to give it back to you until you have reached your goal!

Multiple Savings Pots

Having multiple savings pots for different goals means you can have money slowly building away in the background without you even noticing. This means you can do all sorts of things that you would never have been able to do had you given into the temptation of all those payday treats.

Many more modern banks like Monzo have these kinds of useful budgeting features built in.

If you find it hard to bring yourself to save, there is now a form of passive saving (saving without much conscious effort) that is becoming more common that allows you to drip feed money into a Savings Account or Stocks and Shares ISA. (Don't panic at the thought of the idea of stocks and shares!)

We will look at ISAs and investments in more detail in the Investing chapter and make it nice and simple to understand.

One such application is Moneybox.

This type of saving method is only to be used once you have worked out your budget and are confident that you are able to afford to save and you have established how much you can comfortably put aside. There are quite a few of these available, this is just one example.

You can set a monthly saving amount and then add a weekly boost. This will also take the change from each transaction, round it up to the nearest pound and put it aside for you.

You can put it into cash or invest it into something that might let your money grow more than it would if it was just in a savings account.

Remember when investing, the return you get is not always fixed and, in some cases, you could get back less than you put in. This form of saving is more suited to longer term goals.

Having More Than One Goal

It is likely you will have one goal that you are working towards. This can be managed by working out the time frame for each pot that you set aside, so you will probably want a separate strategy for each pot of money.

We will look at this in the chapter that's coming up, focusing on saving vs investing, and considering different types of short, medium- and long-term goals.

Chapter 3

Saving vs Investing

The traditional wisdom when it comes to money is not to take any risks. However, a more useful way of thinking when it comes to making or growing wealth is that you should learn to manage risks.

Many people struggle with the concept of taking risks when it comes to money. You will often hear people say proudly that they do not take risks with money. What we will look at in this chapter is how not taking any risk with money can be harmful to your financial health. I have spoken to so many clients that tell me when we first meet with absolute certainty that they are not interested in investing at all; they associate the idea of investing with horror stories of people losing all their money that they may have seen in the news or in films like The Wolf of Wall Street.

We all make decisions based on risk dozens of times every day whether it is consciously or not, and it is important to understand the risks associated with saving and investing.

We will look at the risk versus reward concept and look at the difference between saving and investing. One of the things we mentioned in the Budgeting section was the importance of putting some money aside to put towards the goals you set for yourself, be it short term, e.g. a holiday, medium term – purchasing a car, or longer term, such as a deposit for a house or a retirement fund.

Inflation

Inflation is something that is important to understand when it comes to investing.

The American President Ronald Reagan once said, "Inflation is as violent as a mugger, as frightening as an armed robber and as deadly as a hit man." (Keep your wig on Ronnie) While I don't think it's as frightening as a man with a weapon trying to rob you, it's absolutely something worth knowing about.

Example of Inflation in action

Think of a Cadbury's Freddo bar. How much does one cost today? How much did one cost back in the day when you were a young child? The reason for that increase in price is inflation.

Inflation is the rate at which prices of things goes up. In a nutshell, each year the government monitors how much things increase in price each year. Usually in the UK this is between 2% and 3%.

On its own 3% doesn't seem like much, but over the course of many years this really mounts up. Therefore, one of the key things to consider when saving is whether the money you have put aside is keeping up with this rate of inflation. In the last 10 years for example the cost of goods and services increased by 36.4%, based on the Retail Price Index as of December 2020.

Interest

This is the cost of borrowing money. To break it down in a very simple way, if you put money in a savings account, the bank pays you interest for "lending them the money".

However, if you borrow money, the interest is the amount that you pay the bank for their service.

We will look more at the borrowing aspect in the next chapter.

The bank of England sets a rate called the base rate that defines how expensive it is for banks to lend money and the rates they charge customers for lending are supposed to go down as a result.

Banks are businesses that make money from (amongst other things) taking deposits and paying interest to the account holder at a predetermined rate. They also lend money in the form of overdrafts and loans.

This is where they allow their customers to borrow money from the bank and pay a certain amount of interest to the bank for the privilege of doing so.

Interest rates in the UK are currently extremely low. The other thing to keep in mind is that while this base rate is low, the interest the bank will pay you for keeping money in savings accounts will be very low also as the banks aren't making much profit off it.

Saving vs Investing

As we discussed in the Spending section of this book, it is wise to try and keep 3-6 months' worth of earned income set aside in an emergency or "rainy day fund".

This is best kept in an account that will give you immediate access to it when you need it.

Many savings accounts nowadays offer such poor interest returns that if held for a longer time period the buying power of your money will be reduced over time. Think of inflation like termites chewing away at the cash in your account very slowly each year. If you have a longer-term goal that you are saving for, you will want to put your money in a place that will keep pace with inflation.

Leaving money in an account that is losing its buying power is subject to **inflation risk**.

Risk

When we discuss investment, we must consider risk.

This is the reason that any regulated advert relating to investment will have the words "CAPITAL AT RISK YOU MAY GET BACK LESS THAN YOU INVESTED" along the bottom.

There is a very important reason why this is something that must be included; otherwise, the advert might give a misleading representation of how it works.

Some people will naturally associate the work "risk" with opportunity. Others may associate the word with loss. It is important to understand what is meant by risk when we talk about investments.

In an ideal world you would want to be able to make a big return on your investment without any risk. In the real world it is very difficult to get a reward without any risk. This is known as the **risk vs reward** concept.

Any successful business owner will have to have taken a few risks before their business started bringing them in any profit.

Buying a home is a bit of a risk in theory. Having to put down a big deposit, if you lost your income and didn't have any insurance and failed to keep up with your mortgage payments, you could find yourself homeless and you could lose the money you paid in.

These sorts of risks are taken every day as they are common occurrences (buying a home, starting a business etc).

When it comes to investment, broadly speaking low risk investments will offer fairly modest returns.

The more risk that is being taken, the higher the chance of you getting a bigger return.

It is however, a double edged sword, as the higher the level of risk, the chances are, alongside the opportunity for bigger gains, the more likely you would be to see your investment fall in value in the short term. You could even lose all the money you invested.

We will look at the different types of investments available to UK consumers and the risks involved.

When choosing how to invest money, it is important to consider how long you are happy to leave the money invested for, as higher risk investments may take longer to give you that higher reward as higher risk investments are often more **volatile**.

What is Volatility?

Put simply, the amount of volatility is the amount an investment goes up or down in a given period.

SAVING

When working out what investments you should set up for yourself, you can refer to this as your portfolio (if you want to sound fancy) one of these will undoubtedly be a savings account. This allows you to drop in money that you have earned to use later.

Choosing a Savings Account

There are a few things to keep in mind when choosing a savings account. Savings interest is paid tax free, and most people won't have to worry about tax unless you earn more than £1000 a year in interest.

It's important to look at how much interest you will get in return for your deposits and whether there are any terms and conditions that mean you need to keep the money in the account for a certain amount of time, e.g. to achieve a certain interest rate.

Think about the goal you are saving for - let's imagine there is an account that offers a good rate of interest, but it needs you to keep the money in it for over three years to qualify for the higher interest rate, and your goal is buying a car within 18 months. In this case it probably isn't the right product for achieving your goals and you would be better looking at something more flexible.

Although the interest rates are low at the moment, it is worth checking out www.moneysavingexpert.com before you make a choice, because banks offer new products all the time and they usually keep an up-to-date list of what accounts offer the best rates and terms for people with different goals.

Just remember to keep your goal in mind, as well as taking note of the interest rates on offer and the terms and conditions of the accounts.

I won't go into detail on the specific accounts available as I am not trying to advise you to take one over the other, my goal here is simply to educate on the available options and help you determine how to decide what suits your needs best.

The main thing to understand is that with current low interest rates, finding a savings account that will pay more than inflation is regularly paying more than inflation is nearly impossible.

Some accounts will offer eye-catching deals that will pay up to 3% interest for example, providing you switch your bank account to them but then after a year it might drop down significantly.

When it comes to easy access savings accounts, it is difficult to find accounts paying more than 0.5% a year.

Why is it useful to have some investments that offer a higher return than a savings account?

For short term use and ease of access savings accounts are great and easy to use. But what if we had a way of making a bigger return year on year?

For long-term planning you will want to consider the following...

Compounding Interest

Albert Einstein, credited as being the smartest man to have ever lived, once said the following:

"Compound interest is the eighth wonder of the world. He who understands it, earns it. He who doesn't, pays it."

(When I quote this, it makes my colleagues groan as I like to say it so regularly, however my annoying repertoire of things I like to say does not take away from the wisdom of the quote.)

Understanding the beauty of compounding interest is crucial to realising long term investment growth.

It is the concept of interest on interest. I've heard the effect being likened to pushing a snowball down a hill; that it starts off small but as it gathers more snow it gets bigger at a quicker rate as it gathers more size.

I'll give you a simple example to demonstrate. Let's imagine I invest £10,000 today into an account that pays guaranteed 5% interest a year on the anniversary of the investment.

Year	Interest	Total Interest Earned	Balance in £ Pounds
0	-	-	10,000
1	500.00	500	10,500
2	525.00	1025	11025
3	551.25	1576.25	11,576.25
4	578.81	2155.06	12,155.06
5	607.75	2762.82	12,762.82
6	638.14	3400.96	13,400.96
7	670.05	4071.00	14,071.00
8	703.55	4774.55	14,774.55
9	738.73	5513.28	15,513.28
10	775.66	6288.95	16,288.95

As you can see, as the interest mounts up, the addition of that 5% each year is put onto the total balance which includes the invested amount (in this case £10,000) and the previous years' interest and in time the total amount of interest generated allows for a massive level of growth.

This example shows that by achieving 5% growth per year over 10 years, the compounding effect allows the total balance to advance rapidly turning £10,000 into £16,288.95 in 10 years without having to add anything else to the pot.

To achieve inflation beating growth like this, you will need to look to take more risk than just putting it in a savings account. In reality, rather than receiving interest paid out by a bank you would most likely become better off due to the growth of the value of an asset you own. We will have a look at the risks of different types of assets later in the chapter.

Don't Pay Tax on your Savings

You have a choice as to where you put your savings. Under current rules you can earn up to £1000 a year in interest without paying any tax.

As you're starting out, you are likely to be saving relatively small amounts in the beginning therefore tax isn't going to be much of a problem to you. However, it is good practice to get into the mindset of saving in a way where you save 20p on every pound, then by the time you are older and your savings are pots are bulging, then these habits will stop you seeing a load of your hard-earned savings (which you will have potentially already been taxed on) get nabbed by the taxman.

Individual Savings Accounts are the most tax efficient way to save for short- or medium-term goals.

What are ISAs for?

ISAs act like a shield against tax for your savings or investments. Often referred to as a tax wrapper (to wrap around your money or investments to protect them from the tax man).

Outside of an ISA you can earn £1000 interest per year tax free as a basic rate taxpayer, and £500 interest per year as a higher rate taxpayer.

With regards to investments in an ISA, the main problem comes from **Capital Gains Tax** and **Dividend Tax** you must pay when you take your money out.

Capital Gains Tax is payable when you sell an asset you own that has gone up in value since you bought it.

So, for example, if you owned some shares in apple and they increased by 10 times in the time you held them, the tax man would come looking for his cut if you tried to sell them if they weren't inside an ISA.

Dividend tax is payable on dividends produced by stocks.

I won't go into too much more detail on these types of tax here, but it's safe to say you want to try and keep your money inside one of these wrappers to avoid paying these types of tax where possible.

Use your ISA allowances to prevent paying them!

If you are interested, you can find further information on these types of taxes with up-to-date limits here.

https://www.gov.uk/tax-on-dividends

https://www.gov.uk/capital-gains-tax

ISA Allowances

Each ISA type has its own maximum amount you can pay in each year.

Will taking money out affect my allowance?

Some ISA products are more flexible than others.

Some will allow you to take money out and replace it within the same tax year (up to the allowable maximum for that tax year) but some won't.

It's best to check with your provider before you make a withdrawal.

What are the different types of ISAs?

- Junior ISAs
- Cash ISAs
- Stocks and Shares ISAs
- Innovative Finance ISAs and Lifetime ISAs

What is the difference between each type of ISA?

Let's have a look at the different types of accounts and the rules for each one. Remember, the point of these is to allow you to shield your savings/investments from tax. Each one has a maximum limit you can save each year.

JUNIOR ISA

Anyone under 18 in the UK can open a Junior ISA. It is not open to anyone older.

By starting to save early it lets you start building up interest / investment growth over a longer period. The longer you save the more chance you have of achieving your goals earlier in life.

A parent or legal guardian must open this on your behalf. The money cannot be taken out until you turn 18 apart for exceptional circumstances. The money in the account belongs to the child it has been opened for. Granny's birthday tenner can go straight in.... Parents, relatives, and friends can put money in up to an annual limit of **£9000 in 2021/22**. Once paid in it cannot be returned to the person who put it in. Soz granny!

The owner can start to manage it themselves from age 16. No tax is payable by anyone on the growth that is made within the Junior ISA.

Additionally, it's possible to have a **Junior Cash ISA, a Junior Stocks and Shares ISA** or a mix of both as long as the maximum doesn't go beyond £9000.

What happens to my Junior ISA when I turn 18?

You can choose to take it out and spend it how you like. For example, you might want to pay for education, driving lessons or guitar lessons (if you are planning to be a rock star – which is what I should have done at 18).

If you don't go down the international rock star route and would prefer to leave the money invested, it will automatically be rolled over into an adult ISA. Let's have a look at the adult ISAs available.

JUNIOR CASH ISA

This allows you to earn interest on your cash tax free and works like a normal savings account. The only difference is that it is locked in until age 18.

JUNIOR STOCKS AND SHARES ISA

This allows people under 18 to invest in products like bonds or stocks and shares that offer a higher interest rate than cash.

Stocks and shares can go up as well as down so professional advice from a bank or reputable financial adviser should be taken before setting one up, as alongside the risk of it going down there will be charges and other issues to consider. We will look at adult stocks and shares ISAs below.

<u>CASH ISA</u>

These are fairly similar to a savings or buildings society account. You have to be over 18 to set one up however the interest the provider offers will not be taxed. There is no lock in like with junior ISAs.

The maximum you can pay in is £20,000 in any one year – this runs from the 6th April until the 5th April the following year. You can mix up how you allocate that £20,000. We'll look at an example in a moment.

Like with bank/savings accounts, you can do some research as to which one offers the best rates on sites like www.moneysavingexpert.com to see which offers the best return. These are usually covered under the **Financial Services Compensation Scheme** - this is a guarantee of up to £85,000 per account if the bank goes bust.

<u>STOCKS AND SHARES ISAS</u>

You have to be 18 or over to open a Stocks and Shares ISA.

The maximum you can pay in is £20,000 in any one year – this runs from the 6th April until the 5th April the following year. Again, you can mix up how you allocate this £20,000 allowance between your different ISAs.

We're going to look at shares in more detail in the Investing chapter coming up shortly. Sometimes when you own a share of a company, and the company wants to give out a reward to the people who own shares in it (the shareholders) you will get a dividend. When you hold these in a stocks and shares ISA, there will be no tax on any of these little bonuses you get.

You can even buy shares of companies/funds that invest in all sorts of things like property for example, which we will also look at in the Investment section.

As I mentioned before regarding capital gains tax, if you own shares in a company and it increases in value whilst inside a stocks and shares ISA, you can sell this without worrying about tax whenever you want to sell it.

Stocks and Shares ISAs may incur fees. It's a good idea to take professional financial advice before opening any account like this because besides the fees, it has the risk of loss so that you understand how these risks would affect you and whether it matches your goals (reason for investing).

Taking Professional Advice

Stocks and Shares ISAs can be opened for free, and DIY investing companies have exploded over the last few years as young people see the hype online about investing and don't like the idea of having to pay for advice. If it's your first time and you are unsure what you are doing, it is worth consulting a professional. Talking to an adviser doesn't have to be very expensive - many reputable advisers will offer a free consultation and tell you your options without tying you in to buy a product they recommend. Many high street banks can also offer this service for a reasonable price that can often be paid out of your investment.

You can find an adviser by looking on www.vouchedfor.co.uk or www.unbiased.co.uk.

INNOVATIVE FINANCE ISAS

You have to be 18 or over to open an Innovative Finance ISA. The maximum you can pay in is £20,000 in any one year – this runs from the 6th April until the 5th April the following year. Again, you can mix up how you allocate this £20,000 allowance between your different ISAs.

These new style ISAs (IFISA) – are used to hold "peer to peer loans" instead of cash or stocks and shares. This type of loan cuts out the middleman (the banks). Any interest earned would be free of tax.

These are risky and only really aimed at people with a high level of financial knowledge. In actual fact these should only really be used by people who earn a lot of money as they carry the risk of losing all of the money invested. I am covering this type of product just to make sure you understand what it is and are aware of the risks should you ever come across it.

Simplified example – John has 5000 pounds but isn't very excited by the interest rate he is offered by his bank, but a peer-to-peer lender can help by matching him up with Lisa who wants to borrow £5000 but thinks that the rate offered by the peer to peer lender Is better value that the rate she is offered by her bank (as it has a lower APR). John lends her the money at an agreed rate that Lisa is happy with. John would then use the Innovative Finance ISA to store the repayments Lisa makes on the loan and the original £5000 and the interest paid by Lisa would be held free of any tax.

A peer-to-peer loan is a relatively new type of lending/borrowing that matches up investors who want to lend money and get a better return than a standard bank account, with people who want to borrow who might not qualify for lending elsewhere due to their credit file or their age.

Examples of these schemes are run by providers like Zopa or Funding Circle.

They have worked very well to offer some people better value loans than they would have got elsewhere in recent years and do the same things as other lenders like check affordability etc.

The idea of peer-to-peer lending is that the provider matches up investors with people who want to borrow at a lower rate than they might get elsewhere. Users can arrange all this easily online, so there is a lower cost to the provider, potentially a lower rate for the borrower and potentially higher return for the investor.

Innovative ISA big risks

These products are not recommended for less experienced users.

This is because the money borrowed might not be paid back and if the overall scheme collapses, the investors do not have the usual protections they would have in place with more traditional products.

Some providers offer to pay back investors who have lent money that isn't repaid; however, these funds do not guarantee to repay all the money to all of the investors.

The most obvious problem would be if there was a big economic crash and lots of people lost their jobs and did not repay their loans.

Because they are not covered under the **Financial Service Compensation Scheme,** this could cause the lender to fail causing huge losses. For example, a company called Lendy collapsed in 2019 and it meant that 9000 investors were left out of pocket by almost £152 million pounds.

An interesting (but slightly strange) idea from the government, but not really something that would be of much use to most young people, and I would strongly advise that you take professional financial advice if you thought an IFISA might be suitable despite all these risks.

LIFETIME ISA

This is the type of ISA which will be of most interest to people reading this guide. Most young people will have the goal of one day owning their own home and this product can be extremely useful for people trying to achieve this goal.

Known as LISAs, these are designed to help young people aged 18 to 39 to save to buy their first property or save for their retirement.

Benefits of a Lifetime ISA

Using a LISA properly can allow you to earn as much as £32,000 in free cash from the government.

These have been available since April 2017 and replaced the Help to Buy ISA scheme.

How does a LISA work?

For every £4 you put in a LISA, the government will add £1. You can pay up to a maximum of £4000 and the government will top it up by £1000. You can do this every year until you are 50 and you can mix it up with other ISA products so that you can utilise your full £20,000 a year allowance. without any tax applicable at any stage. The bonus is added monthly. It's designed to help you buy your first home or fund your retirement. You must use the money to buy your first house otherwise you will be hit with a 25% deduction unless you keep it until age 60. After age 60, you can take it out and spend it however you like without any penalty.

You need to have the money in the LISA for at least a year before you can use it to fund a deposit, and the property must not cost more than £450,000.

What can I put in a Lifetime ISA?

You can pay in cash (like a cash ISA) or invest in shares (like a stocks and shares ISA).

LISA Risks

It could be tempting to benefit from the growth opportunities of investing in stocks and shares within a LISA.

It is worth remembering that stocks and shares can fall sharply as well as rising, and therefore it may well be more appropriate to just take advantage of the cash LISA and take the 25% bonus each month as this is guaranteed so long as you use it for its intended purpose.

Another risk to keep in mind is that if you have an emergency and need to take money out, you are penalised 25% on the amount you withdraw. This is another reason why it is important to have a separate rainy day or emergency fund that is easily accessible.

Can I transfer a LISA between different providers if I see one with a better rate?

Officially you should be allowed to transfer between different providers relatively easily (within a month), but it is worth checking this with the provider before you open the account because some banks do not currently allow this. You can find more information on Lifetime ISAs here: https://www.moneyadviceservice.org.uk/en/articles/a-guide-to-lifetime-isas.

Chapter 4

Investing

Now that we are looking at investing, we will look at some of the traditional ways that people can invest money to grow their wealth or create a passive income. There are now all sorts of clever ways that you can get access to these different types of investments through easy to access products.

Investing Can Seem Daunting

Some of the concepts in this chapter may seem complicated.

Don't worry if it doesn't all make sense at first. It is simply designed to provide information about how investing can help you grow your savings to help you reach your long-term goals.

Investing isn't scary if you understand investment risk and plan wisely.

This generation of young people will need to have a good understanding of how to increase their wealth if they want to be comfortable later on in life because of cuts to school budgets, increasing house prices, student loans, and the financial circumstances we may find ourselves in as a result of the financial fallout of the Covid pandemic. Getting a good head start in understanding how to invest well will put you in a much stronger position as you begin to face financial challenges.

Important Notice about Investment

It is important for me to state clearly at this point that the information in this chapter is **not financial advice**. I am not recommending one product over another, nor am I recommending any specific investment strategy. This is because no two peoples' circumstances or goals are the same.

I will explain the basics of investment and talk about the potential benefits and risks of different types of investments. This chapter speaks about common strategies and I'm not saying any of these are necessarily the right one for you, I am simply explaining a bit about them to increase your understanding of how many people invest. I hope this will help you develop a decent level of knowledge about your options and what type of products are available on the UK market.

If you want financial advice tailored to your specific goals and circumstances, please speak to a qualified adviser. There is information in the last chapter in this book (Future Planning) on how to seek out high quality affordable professional advice.

How are investment assets usually held?

Investment assets can often be held individually, or you might invest in a group of assets together at once in the form of an Investment Trust or Investment Fund, then you would just use the money you want to invest to buy a portion of this fund.

Ideally you will want to use products like ISAs and pensions as much as possible to minimize the amount of tax payable on your investments.

What is Investment Risk?

There is a certain level of risk associated with each type of investment. This risk is calculated as the likelihood that you could lose money in relation to the return you could expect. Often in investment, the higher the risk, the higher the reward, much like the concept of gambling. However, investment is all about knowing the risks and managing them to make informed decisions.

Most assets will go up and down in value as time goes on. Some will swing up and down more wildly than others. This is referred to as **volatility**.

What are the most common investment assets? What are the risks with each?

An asset that you own is something that has value and may generate future income. There are a range of assets that you can invest in through investment products. Let's have a look at the main asset types, cash as an asset, and property as an asset. Each has a level of risk associated with it.

1. Cash

This asset type is fairly self-explanatory. This is money stored in the form of currency. It will generate the least amount of growth with interest rates being so low, but the value of this asset is not likely to go up and down very much.

Associated Risks. The currency could lose value due to economic conditions – you might see updates on the news saying "the pound has fallen against the dollar or the euro" for example, so this would mean that if you owned a load of pounds sterling, the buying power of your money could reduce.

Also, as I mentioned earlier in my example using the chocolate bar: because of the tiny amount of interest you get paid on savings held as cash for a long time, when the price of things goes up due to inflation, the buying power of your money is reduced.

2. Property

You can own property directly by buying a house/flat, or indirectly by investing in funds that allow you to own a share of a property portfolio. The value of property can go up and down and can generate **a return** through rental income if you own property directly. For example, you own a flat, pay the mortgage of £500 a month, and rent it to someone who pays you £750 a month to live there.

If you own a share of a property portfolio through a product that lets you buy a share of a property portfolio, for example a commercial property fund, and this can give you a pay-out or a "dividend" in return for investing in the asset class.

Associated Risks. Property has a reputation for being a very safe store of value. It is highly thought of in the UK especially as house prices have risen so much in the last 50 years. You will have heard the expression "safe as houses". It is worth knowing that property (much like the stock market) can fall in value for extended periods.

After the 2008 crash UK house prices fell dramatically and took many years to recover their previous value.

Some people who had taken mortgages to buy properties found their mortgages were more than the value of their homes, which is what is called being in "negative equity" – i.e. the "equity" in the property is less that the amount owed on it, so if it was sold the owner would suffer a big loss.

were suspended because of worries the property market would crash if investors panicked and pulled out all their money.

BUY TO LET INVESTMENTS

Taking a mortgage to buy a property directly to rent out can be a great way to have an asset that could increase in value over the long term and produce an income, while someone else pays off the borrowing (mortgage) you took to purchase it.

This can be a great source of **passive income** if done right.

However, it should be noted that this is not always plain sailing, as you are responsible for the upkeep of the property and still need to keep up the mortgage payments even if the tenants do not pay you.

If you were to find yourself in a position where the tenant could not or would not pay, it is often very stressful as you need to keep paying the mortgage and most people don't like the thought of making someone homeless.

Also, it can actually be extremely difficult to evict tenants who decide not to pay. Therefore, this type of investment is only something to consider if you have a source of income large enough to pay the mortgage if no one pays you, and you should have a reserve of funding set aside to pay for incidental payments like repairs or replacing a boiler at short notice etc.

Why Owning Buy to Let Property isn't as Attractive as it Once Was

Alongside the traditional dangers of tenants that don't pay or that trash your property, there are now more reasons why property is no longer as attractive as it once was. The government is trying to reduce the amount of people making big profits from owning several homes and renting them out. Therefore, they have introduced several tax changes to make people reconsider doing this.

With all these changes now in place, owning a second home isn't as profitable as it was in recent history. On buying a second home the amount of **stamp duty** (a tax paid when a property or piece of land is purchased) paid to Her Majesty's Revenue and Customs will now increase.

Since 2020 more income tax is payable on many "Buy to Lets". Previously the interest on the mortgage payments could be deducted from the tax payable on income generated from renting the property. This has now stopped. Also, when you go to sell the property, more tax will have to be paid on the increase in the value of the property since you owned it. So, in a nutshell, more tax on the way in, more tax during ownership and more tax on the way out.

BONDS

Bonds are issued by governments (called gilts) and they are also offered by private companies as a way of raising money. This is essentially you agreeing to lend money to the government or company with an agreement that they will return the money plus a little bit of **interest** at a later date.

Government bonds are thought to be quite safe. The return you get is fairly low compared to other asset types. The return is usually "fixed" so you know how much you will get back after a pre agreed period of time.

Bonds are considered fairly low risk low return – these are designed to form a fairly safe means of getting a fixed return and in many investment strategies the idea is that they can be owned alongside stocks and shares to reduce the **risk** of investing in the stock market.

Bond Risks

Company bonds offer higher returns and the return will most likely be based on how trustworthy the issuer is. These are deemed to be slightly riskier so to compensate you for that risk the rate of return is slightly higher than say a government bond.

This higher return is to compensate you for the risk of the bond issuer going bust and not being able to pay you back your money.

It should be kept in mind that when the price of a bond is set it takes into account the current **interest rates** so if interest rates rise the value of the bond can go down.

STOCKS AND SHARES

What exactly is a "Share"?

When you buy a share, you are buying a portion of a company. Investing in stocks and shares has traditionally been a route to growing your wealth. Offering shares of a company is a very common way for businesses to raise money. These are bought and sold on a particular **stock exchange.**

What is the Stock Market?

The stock market is where investors come together to buy and sell and trade shares in companies.

You may have heard of the "FTSE" (pronounced footsie). This is the UK's stock exchange. The full title is the Financial Times Stock Exchange.

There are different **"indexes"** which group together a broad range of different types of shares. The FTSE 100 is an index which shows you the 100 biggest UK stocks.

Another **index** would be the FTSE 250 which shows you the top 250 companies and so on. There are different markets all around the world that allow people to buy and sell shares of companies.

Each big **economy** has its own Stock Exchange (UK, US, Germany, Japan etc).

It is important to understand that the value of a share might not always directly relate to how successful or profitable the company is.

Unless you are an expert, if you are to invest in stocks and shares it is wise to invest in a range of different shares. "Not putting all your eggs in one basket" is important here.

Investing in stocks and shares is really only suitable for long term investment due to how much these assets can go up and down.

For example, if you were starting a pension at 20, having a lot of it in well invested stocks and shares mightn't be a bad thing as they will swing up and down but historically have generated high returns and the volatility shouldn't be too much of a concern because the earliest you can access it is when you are 57 (under current rules).

Therefore, this gives you plenty of time to allow it to allow the market to swing back up again if it falls.

Stock Market Returns

The S&P 500 is a list of the top 500 companies in the United States. The companies within it will change on a regular basis as stocks rise and fall. Since the 1920s, this has grown by an average of around 10%. Remember this is not to say every company in the top 500 companies will increase in value by 10% a year. Some will perform badly and be replaced by other companies that perform better as time goes on.

There are many investment funds that allow you to own a portion of each company in a particular **stock market index**. These are called **tracker funds** and will allow your investment to track a particular economy. You can even get "global" trackers where you can own shares in up to 23 developed economies at once.

The UK stock market the FTSE 100 has returned an average of around 7% or 8% each year since it was set up. This is an **average**. Some years it will go up much more than this, and some years it will go down considerably. This type of investing is the most common way to create big gains over the long term. As I mentioned just now, most pension schemes will contain a large amount of investment in the stock market for example.

Stocks and Shares Risks

More and more young people are getting involved in investing in the stock market. Some of this interest is due to TikTok/Instagram stock market gurus and adverts that give the impression that they are like a bet that you can't lose.

I think it is great that young people are becoming interested in investment for the long term however it must be said that stock market investment does involve risks. One important point to note is that stocks and shares investments are not suitable for short term investment - if you look at the Covid period as an example, the UK stock market fell by 30% in the space of a few weeks. Although it went back up again on this occasion, the recovery could have been much slower.

In the case of the Coronavirus, many individual companies went bust as the stock market fell. Investing in individual shares is much riskier than a fund that contains a range of different shares as there are external factors you have no control of that can massively affect the value of a share.

STOCKS AND SHARES ISAS

Stocks and Shares ISAs are available to anyone over 18. These are amazing products that allow anyone over the age of 18 to invest in stocks and shares. They allow you to pay up to £20,000 every year tax free into a range of different assets.   There is no tax on the money going in, no tax on the growth and no tax when you take money out. You can invest in investment trusts, investment funds, individual shares, government bonds or company bonds.

What to put in a Stocks and Shares ISA?

We looked at these in the previous chapter, but for now we will look at what stocks and shares you can put in this type of ISA. You can put in all types of shares, including shares of funds that invest in assets thought to be safer e.g. bonds or commercial property, even gold!

Stocks and Shares ISAs are an awesome way to beat inflation and save for the long term. You could put individual stocks in a Stocks and Shares ISA, but this carries a lot of risk. If the company you've invested in goes down the toilet, so does your investment.

When it comes to saving in Stocks and Shares ISAs, it's best to get a collection of stocks and shares to spread the risk (diversify) across a range of different product/service types.

Unless you are a highly skilled stock analyst it's probably best leaving the selection of these funds to someone else who does this for a living.   There are a couple of different approaches for investing, which we will look into now.

PASSIVE VS ACTIVE INVESTING

You can buy shares in funds that invest your money for you and buy stocks and shares on your behalf for a small fee.

Many people Use Index funds, Unit Trusts or Investment Trusts to let someone else manage the investments on their behalf so that it matches their goals and willingness to take investment risk.

Active Funds

Some investment funds will choose a selection of shares for you. Take for example a very popular actively managed UK fund run by investment manager Terry Smith, Fundsmith. Fundsmith is an Investment Trust. This allows you to pool your money with other investors and use it to invest in a range of shares such as Microsoft, Paypal, L'Oreal and dozens of others. You pay them a management charge each year to manage these investments and change them in line with their research.

Past performance is no guide to future returns so you cannot bank on it repeating any success. Between March 2011 and March 2021 Fundsmith increased in value by 429%. This example has been a massive success but there is no guarantee this will happen again in the next 10 years.

The success or failure of these funds will be down to the choices the managers make. They will study trends and company research. Ultimately, a lot of it will boil down to luck as the managers are ultimately making guesses based on their research but they do not have a crystal ball and do not know what will happen in the future.

Active Fund Costs

The cost for this management can be very high, averaging at around 1.5% of the investment per year. This is taken whether the fund drops or increases.

Active Fund Risks

You are leaving a manager (usually a team of managers) in charge of making decisions on your behalf. Some may have a really good run for years making good investments, but then make errors in judgement which could cost you dearly. Therefore, it is important to carefully research any active fund you invest in and take good advice before doing so. Some people prefer the idea of having active management during uncertain times as the managers can chop and change the investment strategy regularly to increase short term performance. However, statistics show that over extended periods of time, very few active funds consistently outperform passive funds.

Passive Funds

Passive investment relies on just investing a little bit of your money in each of the top companies in a particular **index** (like the FTSE or S&P 500). One of the most famous passive investment managers Jack Bogle once summed it up by saying "Don't look for the needle in the haystack. Just buy the haystack."

This method of investing is much cheaper because it simply replicates a list of shares that appear in the stock exchange so doesn't require much research or administration etc. This reduced cost can have a massive impact on the overall performance of the investment.

Passive Fund Costs

The average passive fund charge is around 0.15% per year so it is extremely cheap in comparison to active funds which will charge at a much higher level because they have to pay the investment managers and fund the research etc.

Passive Fund Risks

If your fund is blindly tracking a particular market (for example the UK stock market), something that reduces confidence in the economy such as Brexit or Covid could come along and the entire market could drop, meaning you have to wait for it to recover to see your fund perform well again.

Some people prefer the idea of having someone making shrewd decisions on their behalf during a crisis to steer the ship in a particular way, taking advantage of market drops to research and buy shares they believe to be undervalued to make them a much better short term return.

Active vs Passive Investment Products

There is a very long running debate around which style of investment is better.

Active funds might perform much better than passive funds for a short period of time due to good management and a dash of good luck, but if the managers get things wrong, they can then find their funds running into serious trouble.

For example, there was a star manager called Neil Woodford who was accepted as being one of the greatest UK investment managers for a very long time, but in 2019 he had to suspend his flagship fund due to alleged mistakes he had made in his investment strategy.

Passive funds are much cheaper and simply go with the flow. A piece of research done by Vanguard, a huge passive fund manager, shows that only 18% of active fund managers beat their passive rivals over a 15-year period. Picking that fund that is going to be one of the 18% is going to be very difficult without a great deal of insight and a bit of luck.

Popular Beginner Strategies for Long Term Investing

If you are looking at putting money aside for retirement or a long-term goal, then short-term volatility should not really bother you too much.

The most famous investor of all time is Warren Buffett. He is one of the most successful investors of the 20th century, having built up a fortune of $89 billion. He invests in an "active" manner, buying and selling as opportunities present themselves. In "The Little Book of Common Sense Investing", he told the author "A low-cost index fund is the most sensible equity (stocks and shares) investment for the great majority of investors."

An index fund just automatically buys the shares in a particular index like the S&P 500 or the FTSE 100. The holdings will update regularly so that you are always invested in the best performing shares, cutting out the dead wood regularly.

"By periodically investing in an index fund, the know-nothing investor can actually out-perform most investment professionals," Buffett said.

The idea behind this is that when it comes to investing there are certain things you can control and some things you can't.

You can't control what happens in the stock market, but if you keep investing regularly and stay invested long enough, the idea is that the fund will ride out the ups and downs of the markets and leave you a healthy amount of money for your long-term goals.

Understanding your Attitude to Investment Risk

If you develop a good understanding of how investment works, you will understand that taking risks is crucial to meeting your long-term goals. However even with this knowledge, you may well be someone who gets very nervous when you see your investments drop considerably.

If this is the case, and the thought of short-term losses would cause you sleepless nights, you may want to think carefully about investing too heavily in stocks and shares as this is part and parcel of stock market investing.

If you aren't too concerned about getting the best possible return over the long term and would rather see your money grow in a more gradual way, then you might want to look for a portfolio that has a bigger mix of asset types.

More information on working out your appetite for risk can be found here:

https://www.moneyadviceservice.org.uk/en/articles/know-your-risk-appetite#how-to-assess-your-risk-appetite

Speak to a well-qualified financial adviser and they will be able to set you up with an investment strategy that meets your needs. You can find a good financial adviser using www.unbiased.co.uk.

Using this site, you will see 27,000 regulated financial advisers based all over the UK.

Many of these will have a free consultation but be aware they will ultimately be looking to get paid for setting up certain products, so shop around to ensure you are getting a good deal.

Additionally, don't be afraid to challenge them on their charges and the charges associated with products they recommend. The adviser will be required to talk you through these if they are to comply with regulations.

LIFESTYLING

A common strategy when investing for the long term is to use a method called **lifestyling.**

Lifestyling is a method of investing where the amount of risk being taken with your investments is more focused on growth in your earlier years (investing heavily in stocks and shares).

The ups and downs in the early years aren't too much of a concern because you won't have a lot set aside and the money isn't required for many years to come. As you approach the date at which you want to spend the money, the investment strategy changes to become more cautious, swapping the stocks and shares for less volatile assets like bonds and cash.

CRYPTOCURRENCY

There has been a lot of media attention around cryptocurrencies in the last few years.

Many high-profile celebrities and influential people have made the news for making predictions about Bitcoin, Ethereum and Dogecoin etc.

The financial watchdog the Financial Conduct Authority have expressed concern about the startling rise in young people putting money into these very risky investments.

What is Cryptocurrency?

It is a store of value created and held online. There is no actual underlying physical asset that you own when you hold any cryptocurrency.

Satoshi Nakamoto, Bitcoin's inventor, designed it as a way to allow regular transactions to take place in private. It was set up to get around the systems and checks built into traditional banking after the financial crash in 2008.

These "coins" can be used as a way to purchase items online and it was historically linked to black market transactions. They are increasingly being used as investment assets, but as of this time a lot of them are very early in their development. This means they are open to fraud and manipulation. They rise and fall very sharply so need to be treated with extreme caution.

Should I invest in Crypto?

In an FCA-commissioned report in March 2021, researchers uncovered a "striking" lack of awareness of the dangers associated with investing, with 45% of those questioned not viewing "losing some money" as a potential risk. This means almost half the people responding did not seem concerned that they could lose some or all of their money. This is very worrying as the adverts you see online often only tell you about how much you could increase your wealth through these coins.

At this time, cryptocurrencies are just too unstable to justify putting in large sums of money as part of a long-term plan, due to the massive amount of risk involved. There is a possibility at some point in the future this outlook could change when these currencies become more stable.

There are efforts being made as we speak to make them more regulated and more checks and balances are being put in place.

Some respected economists are forecasting that in the future, having a small amount of your savings stored in Cryptocurrency could be the norm, much like people in this day in age own gold as an alternative store of value.

As things stand right now, you should be prepared to lose any money that you put into cryptocurrency, as this is a very risky way to invest.

Especially with the new so-called altcoins that pop up with a lot of hype surrounding them from week to week.

Crypto Highs and Lows

To give you an example of the highs and lows, in 2011 the worth of each Bitcoin soared from a value of $1 in April to a peak of $32 in June. This massive spike in value led a lot of people to believe they had found the goose that lays golden eggs.   Some reports online even describe how some people sold their homes to put all the money they could get their hands on into Bitcoin to make themselves rich beyond their wildest dreams. Unfortunately, the price crashed soon after and had dropped from a high of $32 in June down to just $2 by November 2011. Yikes.

Crypto Scams

There is a lot of misleading information being directed at unsuspecting young adults by people who have disclosed interests in these schemes. For example, these "gurus" may be orchestrating sharp rises in the value of the currency by hyping up how much money it will make investors on social media platforms.

As the price rises, people see the value of their money rise, then get tempted to put in more than they can afford.

These same gurus that created the hype will sell off their own coins and pocket a tidy profit before the value crashes leaving a lot of unsuspecting investors holding the bag.

AVOIDING SCAMS

What are they?

A scam is an attempt to take your money off you using dishonesty.

These schemes come in all shapes and sizes, from the very basic, poorly translated blackmail emails asking for money in order to stop embarrassing videos of you being released to your friends and family, to highly sophisticated schemes involving cloned websites and bogus call centres set up to steal your identity and sell it on the dark web.

These can be a bit of a mild annoyance but if they catch you out it can cause major problems to your life. For example, I have spoken to many hardworking people who lost many thousands of pounds to pension scammers because they were targeted by these immoral people.

Scams have unfortunately become so common that all you need to do is open your email inbox or check the messages on your phone and it is likely that you will find a message from someone pretending to be someone else attempting to trick you into handing over valuable information.

According to the Citizens Advice Bureau, up to four million people are the victims of fraud each year in the UK.

What has caused this rise in fraud cases?

It seems that since the first Covid lockdown in 2020, the scams have gone through the roof.

The crisis created the perfect conditions for scam artists to operate, as more and more people were confined to their homes with their phones at arm's reach.

With millions of people around the world out of work, organised gangs turn to fraud and use some people's naivety and desperation to their advantage in order to swindle them out of money.

What sort of scams are most common?

The Citizens Advice Bureau and Action Fraud did some research into the rise in fraud and gave the following statistics:

- 34% of scams were conducted over the phone (voice calls)
- Almost a quarter (24%) of scams were as the result of a visit to a website
- 16% were as a result of letters and faxes sent to victims' homes
- One in 10 were carried out through email.

What can I do to avoid being scammed?

- If you get a call, text or email out of the blue, be suspicious. If someone says they are calling from a particular agency you should check with the actual organisation and contact them back on a number you know to be correct.
- Change your passwords regularly and do not make them easy to guess. Use a mix of letters and numbers like for example "F1n@ncialHealth!". Try to use a different password for each site as if one gets compromised, a scammer could use your email address to use that same password to try and get on dozens of other sites.
- Never give out personal information like bank PIN codes – your bank will never ask for that information. Nor will they ever come to collect your card from you via courier for any reason.
- If you are shopping online, look for the https next to the address. This means it is secure and that your payment details will be protected while the transaction is carried out.
- If you get an email from a company, use your email browser to check the actual address it has come from. Many scammers will send from addresses that look similar to the company domain they are claiming to be from, but with a slight change hoping you won't notice.

An example of this would be info@aapple.com (pretending to be from Apple), or fraudteam@barclaysbankk.com (pretending to be from Barclays).

- Use an antivirus security tool like McAfee, Avast or Norton 360. Many of these will block harmful sites and stop you from accidentally downloading a virus or something that will send your details to hackers.

Ultimately, the number one rule to keep in mind is 'if it seems too good to be true, it probably is'.

What do I do if I think I have been a victim of a scammer?

You should contact *Action Fraud* straight away if you feel you have been a victim of fraud. They work with the police to shut down fraudsters and offer support to people who have been victims of fraud and cybercrime. *Action Fraud* is the UK's dedicated service for reporting fraud or suspected scams.

They can be contacted at https://www.actionfraud.police.uk/

or by calling 0300 123 2040.

If your bank details have been compromised, contact your bank straight away and let them know. They have fraud teams who are set up to help you and can block your card to stop further transactions.

Chapter 5

Borrowing and Debt

Not all debt is created equal, and not all debt is something to be fearful of. It's important that you understand how borrowing works, how it can be used to your advantage in some situations, and how not to fall into debt that you cannot manage.

Debt, also referred to as credit, is the concept of owing something to someone.

If you have read the Spending chapter, you will know that ideally you should try and keep a "rainy day fund" that you can use rather than getting into debt when you don't need to.

The reality is that in most cases getting through life without some debt is unlikely.

The problem with borrowing is that it needs to be paid back sometime, and when you take on more than you can handle it can spiral out of control and lead to a lot of stress down the line.

In some cases, debts that go bad can cause you long term financial problems, even going as far as to affect the jobs you can get or your eligibility to own your own home.

Debt can be thought of like a time machine, in that it's just saving in reverse. You can use debt to get something immediately that you will pay for later. There is a certain amount of risk here because if your situation changes and you can't keep up your repayments, you will have a lot of hassle. Lenders will allow you to borrow money and charge you interest for the privilege.

Let's look at an example:

You buy a car that costs £5000. You haven't got that amount saved up, but you need the car immediately.

The bank will lend you £5000 and you tell them you can pay it back in monthly instalments. You speak to the bank and tell them how much you can afford to pay back each month. They check up on your history and decide whether to lend to you.

They are satisfied that it is safe to lend you this sum based on what information they find out. They agree to lend you the amount and you agree to pay them back over 5 years. They will charge you an additional £524 so that you pay back £5524 in total. That £524 is the amount of interest.

The way lenders decide how expensive it is to borrow is by using an APR - Annual Percentage Rate.

This is essentially a way of seeing how much it will cost you in total per year to borrow using the product and allowing you to compare between different lending products.

According to the Office of National Statistics, as of November 2020 the average household in the UK owes £60,720 including £2,133 spent on credit cards.

What are the Most Common Types of Debt for Young People?

Credit cards, overdrafts, store cards, personal loans and mortgages are historically the most common form of debt that young people deal with. In recent times however there has also been a rise of companies that let you pay for products in instalments such as *Klarna* and *Clearpay*.

In this chapter we will look primarily at what is known as "unsecured debt". That is money you owe that is not "secured" against a home.

Alternatively, if you have secured debt then you are borrowing against your home. This is much more serious, as when you can't keep up the payments on secured debt it can result in losing your house.

Usually, the most troublesome form of debt for young people is unsecured debt like credit cards and increasingly through unregulated products that allow you to pay back larger sums in instalments.

"A Gucci bag like the one my favourite musician put up on Instagram! Wow! Oh, hold on it's £700. I can't afford that... Wait? What does that say? I can pay it back in instalments of £100? I can just about afford that! Get in! I'll buy it." If that thought process sounds familiar to you, stop what you're doing. You need to strap yourself in and prepare to read this chapter very carefully.

How do young people get into problem debt?

First and foremost - credit cards and store cards are NOT a source of free money. Credit card companies want you to spend their money. The reason for this is because they are businesses like any other, and as such they are always looking to make a profit - they make money when people take out their cards and don't manage them properly!

Mistakes made with credit cards, store cards and same-day lenders can follow you around for a long time, leaving a harsh mark on your credit file for years to come.

Money problems such as missed payments and owing money to a number of different organisations may seem like just a short-term inconvenience right now, but banks and credit card companies use this kind of data collected in your credit file to work out how much interest to charge you when you need to borrow money down the line. Long story short, the worse your credit score is when they assess you, the higher the interest rate you will be charged.

Their reasoning might go something like this - "Fergal has a history of late repayments and didn't repay his phone bill for three months last year, so we don't really feel he is trustworthy to pay the money back. We are going to charge him more because based on this information we have on Feargal, it seems like a RISK on our part to lend money to him."

This score, alongside other additional criteria, are what they will take into consideration when they decide how "creditworthy" you are. The lender might even decide it's too risky based on your previous behaviour and refuse to loan you any money at all.

CREDIT FILES

What is a Credit File?

A credit file is a central database of information stored about each person who is financially active in the country. This information is compiled by companies known as Credit Reference Agencies (CRAs), and in the UK the three main CRAs are Equifax, Experian and TransUnion.

These companies hold a record of almost every application you make for credit; everything from your first mobile phone contract to your home's mortgage is on your credit file.

It is important to try and maintain your credit score, keeping it as high as possible as this will mean that you can qualify for better deals when you need to borrow money.

If you miss payments or fall very far behind, this is recorded. Missing several payments can cause a payment to be deemed as a "default" or a bad debt against your name that will stay on your credit file for 7 years. (Yes, you heard that right! 7 whole years.)

You would think that if you have never borrowed money or missed payments on anything, your credit file will be perfect, right?

Unfortunately not. If the credit reference agency has no record of you, they will not recommend you to lenders as there is nothing there to demonstrate that you are good at keeping up with payments.

How Can I Check My Credit File?

There are companies that allow you to check this for free. *Experian, Clearscore* and *Noddle* allow you to check this online for free.

Some companies will allow you a 30 day trial period then charge you after, so if you use one of these, make sure you cancel before the 30 days is up unless you want to pay to keep an account open. Experian is probably the most accurate and easy to use service.

Some of the other companies, whilst free, will tell you your score needs improvement when there might not be anything wrong with it - they will make an offer to help you improve it if you pay them a fee each month.

How Can I Improve My Credit File?

Tip 1. Check your credit score. You can do this for free online using any of the websites outlined above (*Noddle, Clearscore* and *Experian*) although there are others out there.

Tip 2. Keep up to date with all your payments, as phone/utility bills can affect your score.

Tip 3. Register on the electoral roll (voting register) with your local council.

Tip 4. If your score is low because you haven't had any credit, you should take out a credit card. Some banks offer "credit builder" cards - you can use your card to buy one or two things each month   (things that you would normally have bought with your debit card) and clear these off when the bill is due before interest is payable.

Doing this will show that you can be trusted to repay debt and your score will go up like magic. Just remember not to let the debt sit on the balance sheet. Get it paid off!

Tip 5. If there is any incorrect information on the credit file, this could be impacting your score negatively.

Contact the company or council relating to that information and apply for a "notice of correction" - this should sort the problem out.

Tip 6. Do not open a joint account with anyone that you do not trust 100%. If they run up a debt and your name is on the account this can ruin your credit as you will be held equally as liable, even if you no longer have any connection to the person! So be very careful who you open accounts with.

Tip 7. If you have unpaid debts showing on your credit file, contact the company you owe money to and work out a payment plan so that it shows as settled.

PAYING OFF DEBT

Not having any debt is a nice feeling. If you have found yourself owing a lot of money, getting it paid off really lifts a weight off your shoulders.

There are different approaches to take when looking at clearing off debt - resolving debt is possible as long as you have a plan in place, and you stick to it. If it is unmanageable levels of debt you have found yourself in, there are people you can speak to for free to help you resolve it another way by setting up a payment plan, debt relief order or IVA (e.g. with *StepChange,* who we will talk about in more detail in the next chapter).

Luckily there are no debtor's prisons in this country anymore, so the worst-case scenario isn't really all that bad, so just deal with the debt head on and don't bury your head in the sand. The best strategy for paying off debt is looking at what you owe and clearing off high interest debts first and then working your way down the list.

A good strategy is to clear off the debt with the highest APR (rate of interest) first. The reason for this is that this debt will be the hardest to clear off as this will be the amount that goes down the slowest each time you make a payment. This is due to the fact that a lot of the payment you make will disappear (to pay the interest) leaving the more of money you originally borrowed still outstanding.

If your credit score is okay, and you have a few different debts, for example, including overdrafts and credit cards etc you may qualify for a loan that would have a lower APR (annual percentage rate).

You could look at working out how much you owe in total. Then you could see if it is possible to get a loan to clear all of it at potentially a lower interest rate.

Just be careful not to run a high number of credit checks/applications in a short period of time, as this can actually negatively affect your score.

<u>Here's an example of how a consolidation loan could be of use:</u>

John is fed up with debt. He has no savings. He has a current account with a £1000 overdraft he built up when he was a student that charges 18% APR for all the time he spends in his overdraft, and because he earns £1600 a month, he is using his overdraft all the time because when he gets paid his bills are £700 which takes him into his overdraft straight away each month.

John has a credit card on which he owes £3000. The credit card interest rate is 16.9% APR. He keeps meaning to clear it but finds it easier to just pay the minimum payment of about £40 each month.

He has checked on Experian and his credit file is very good as he always makes his payments and is on the electoral roll and has no debts that have ever been left unpaid.

He researched the market using a comparison site and found that he can get a loan for £4000 which he can use to clear both the overdraft and the credit card. The interest rate is much lower, coming in at 6%. He works out looking at his budget, he can afford to pay around £120 a month.

His problem currently is that the overdraft would need him to either clear the whole thing at once (which he can't afford to do) or be very careful to leave a surplus each month until he reduces his overdraft to zero.

This can be tricky to keep an eye on and leaves the temptation to just use it all each month. The credit card company is happy for him to keep paying the minimum payment each month so in theory he could go on paying both of these forever, paying many thousands of pounds in interest as the years go by.

The loan would enable him to be debt free in 36 months. The advantage is that he can set it up to come out on the day he gets paid and he doesn't have the temptation to pay less as the repayments are fixed. Some loan companies will even agree to payment holidays in the event of financial difficulties but speak to the lender before making any decisions to this and be aware of any negative impact of taking one. The loan would mean that he pays a total of £370.40 in interest payments. In this example this would be a great result for John as paying interest over long periods of time can really damage your financial health. Let's have a look at why it is important to pay more than the minimum payment towards these "rolling" debts.

Paying off your credit/store card

As mentioned before, a credit card is a good thing to have. It can allow you some legal protection for large payments that debit cards don't offer.

Some cards also offer interest free periods which can be useful for booking things like holidays in case things don't go to plan - you may be able to claim it back. However, if you don't manage these payments properly, you may find yourself spiralling into problems.

Do not just pay the minimum payment – try and clear off credit card debt as soon as possible. Additionally, keep your eye on your balance! If you signed up to a card with an interest free period, after this ends you will go onto their standard rate which could be very high.

Therefore, if you are approaching the end of the interest free period, try to swap it to another card that offers an interest free period to avoid paying high rates of interest. This is called a balance transfer. The average credit card charges about 18% APR so try not to fall into paying this.

If you pay by direct debit this will make it less likely to forget and miss a payment, as these missed payments can haunt you for a long time.

Remember to pay your priority debts first. If you find yourself struggling with debt, do not bury your head in the sand, go and speak to your creditors. Many offer payment holidays and can offer short term help. There is plenty of information on how to deal with problem debt in the chapter on Mental Health and Financial Wellbeing.

Pay in Instalment Options – "Death by 1000 Cuts"

In the last couple of years, many companies have started offering you the option to pay in instalments.

According to a study carried out by Chris Woolard for the Financial Conduct Authority (FCA), the use of these unregulated "Buy Now, Pay Later" (BNPL) products have nearly quadrupled in 2020. Additionally, data provided by some BNPL providers indicates that a quarter of users are between the ages of 18 to 24.

With so many popular young "influencers" and YouTubers being paid to advertise expensive clothes online, it's easy to see why BNPL programmes are becoming so desirable. The reality however is that most of the time these items are given to these already-wealthy influencers for free and are often unaffordable for the vast majority of people actually seeing the ads.

A lot of these deferred payment products are pushed very hard on social media. You know the ones I mean... You'll see them at the point when you get to the checkout on an online store and get hit with the enticing offer to pay for your purchase in instalments without paying any interest.

It makes that overpriced £170 pair of trainers seem so much more affordable if you can pay just £30 a month until they're paid off.

These companies are getting a lot of bad press (and rightly so in my opinion) because they often do not perform any affordability checks or credit checks on their customer base, therefore making it very easy for young people to run up debts of thousands that they cannot afford, landing them in severe financial difficulties.

This is the reason why these offers are dangerous – having no affordability check means that they have no idea whether you have no money coming in to be able to make these repayments. In addition, they allow you to borrow from several of these lenders at once which just compounds the risk. Online shopping can seem like it isn't real because you aren't handing over your debit card or handing anyone cash; just daydreaming on the bus clicking a few buttons in a trance looking at all the items you want and think you need. On this note, the same FCA study showed that 90% of transactions made using BNPL services involved fashion and footwear.

Before you know it, you could end up paying for a shedload of overpriced items that you wouldn't have bought if you had to pay all at once.

These might also come out at different times throughout the month, making it even more difficult for you to budget.

Be careful and think very carefully before using these "offers".

Keep in mind that some lenders will check your spending habits before deciding whether or not to lend to you, and if they see lots of high-risk borrowing, they may well decide not to lend you any money.

GOOD DEBT VS BAD DEBT

Good Debt

Put very simply, what we refer to as "Good Debt" is borrowing that will put you in a better financial position in the long run.

What type of transactions might be considered "good" debt?

- Self-Improvement – if you have borrowed money to go towards learning a skill that could get you a better job or make you some income in the future this would be seen as a good reason to borrow.
- Buying a car/other vehicle – you might need to buy a vehicle to become successful. Cars (and paying for fuel / insurance tax etc) can be expensive. That being said, if you were to buy an affordable car it could really improve the quality of your life with regards to employment and experiences you would otherwise have to miss out on.
- Mortgages – if you don't have the money to buy a house right out, then getting a mortgage will likely be your only way of owning a home.

We will look at the benefits of home ownership a bit later on in this guide, but say you borrowed some money to own a second home and then someone was willing to pay you rent of more than the original repayments, you would now have an asset that generates income.

House prices can go up and down, but generally speaking if you buy a house in a nice area, once the mortgage is paid off, the property will probably be worth more than what you paid for it in the first place. Therefore, using borrowing in this example would allow you to own an asset that not only pays you an income but also increases in value. Once you own it in full, you can continue to take income from the property in the form of rent or by selling it.

Bad Debt

While debt for a worthy purpose that puts you in a better position can be useful in some circumstances, getting into debt where it is unnecessary is never a good idea.

You should avoid getting into debt if this is being taken out to purchase something you don't absolutely need. Although with all the pressure from social media and targeted ads, it can sometimes feel like you are the only one not wearing the latest clothes or going to exotic places on holiday.

Assess all of your purchases taken out on credit before you make them and assess them harshly - if it's for short term enjoyment at the expense of long term payments at a high interest rate, you should probably reconsider your purchase.

HIGH INTEREST LOANS

Many companies have sprung up across the UK looking to make money from people with poor credit history and perhaps little understanding of how lending works. When payments are missed the interest can roll up making it impossible to catch up.

These companies often end up being closed down by the regulators, however they may be operational for several years causing untold misery before they get shut down.

Payday Loans

These types of loans are to be avoided if at all possible. They are designed to provide short term cash to tide you over until payday.

They might seem like they are offering fairly cheap lending due to the short period of time that the money is actually being borrowed, however these debts can very easily spiral out of control, as the affordability checks may not always be as tight as they should be.

Once the money remains unpaid for any considerable length of time it can rack up huge rates of interest, and because they are intended to be paid off in a few weeks the APR on these loans can be higher than 1000%. This means that as soon as your unpaid debt starts to rack up interest the cost can quickly become totally unmanageable. This is especially dangerous as in the future, other lenders may decline mortgages or more reasonable loans if they see evidence of high interest lending on your bank statement, because to them it signifies a history of financial difficulty or lack of knowledge with regards to managing finance.

Debt to Pay for Everyday Items

If you find you are finding yourself borrowing regularly to pay for daily items, make sure you have gone through your budget carefully to see if there are any areas where you are overspending.

If you find that you are still needing to borrow, you should speak to your local Citizens Advice Bureau to see if you are eligible for any state benefits. If you are struggling, talk to friends and family about your situation, and speak to free professional debt advice specialists like *StepChange* who can be contacted on 0800 138 1111.

Chapter 6
Mental Health and Financial Wellbeing

Our modern world is filled with pressure and stress for young people, and there is a clear link between mental health issues and financial problems. You may not realise it but establishing a healthy relationship with money and becoming financially literate can also help with improving your mental health and wellbeing.

Mental health issues are common, and financial issues are often a factor that can cause mental health problems or make these issues more serious.

A survey carried out by the Money and Mental Health Institute in 2016 found that 86% of respondents believed their financial situation had made their mental health problems worse. Additionally, 46% of people in problem debt said they have suffered from mental health problems.

Part of managing your mental health is accepting that there are some things in life we will never be able to control – the weather outside or the untimely passing of a loved one – but you needn't let your finances be one of these uncontrollable situations.

The first step to financial wellbeing is to adopt a proactive mindset and work to improve your situation by taking action.

Dangers for "The Lost Generation"

Having grown up through a pandemic and job losses that affected young people more than any other age group, the future can seem pretty bleak for people growing up in today's economic landscape.

Extended periods of austerity (reduced government spending) and lockdowns create high-risk conditions for sufferers of mental illness.

It's no mystery why many young people might experience feelings of hopelessness, but the worst thing you can do is suffer in silence. The old saying "A problem shared is a problem halved" has a lot of truth in it; when your mood is low and your mindset is gloomy, seeking a second opinion from someone who has your best interests at heart is often the best thing you can do. Burying your head in the sand and hoping things will sort themselves out simply doesn't work.

Aim to develop a mindset that allows you to take a step back every so often, take a deep breath, and assess your situation rationally. If you're not in the place to do this right now, consider talking about any concerns with someone you trust, and who you feel has a good handle on their own finances.

The UK government runs a helpful scheme called the *Money Advice Service*, although at time of writing it's currently changing its name to the *Money and Pensions Service*.

They can help by breaking down complicated financial issues into easy to understand language. They are available for support Monday to Friday, from 8am to 6pm by calling 0800 138 7777.

What are mental health issues and how do they affect young people?

When people talk about mental health, they're referring to your state of mind.

Questions to consider when thinking about your mental health are "Do I feel that I am able to cope with day-to-day life?", "Do I feel positive about who I am and what I can achieve?", and "Do I feel connected to those around me?"

There are a lot of things we can do to look after our general mental health, such as getting enough sleep and keeping in touch with friends and family, but sometimes we suffer from mental health issues that are much more difficult to manage and often require input from a medical professional.

The two most common of these issues are **depression and anxiety**.

Mind Wise are a charity who do amazing work in helping support people with mental health issues. I am going to link to some of the amazing resources they offer throughout this chapter.

I am just going to talk about some of the most common issues that go hand in hand with financial struggles, however they offer advice and support on a wide range of issues. Find them here: https://www.mindwisenv.org/

What is Depression?

Depression is a mental health condition that affects almost 20% of people aged 16 or older in the UK. It is an issue that can be occasional or more persistent that presents symptoms of:

- Low mood
- Hopelessness
- Low self-esteem
- Strong feelings of guilt

- Lack of motivation
- Suicidal thoughts

Not everyone who suffers from depression displays all of these symptoms, some sufferers may only show one or two symptoms.

Identifying clinical depression from general sadness is difficult, however.

Getting a diagnosis means showing symptoms over a long period in a way which affects your day-to-day life, for example if how you feel begins to impact on your relationships or on your career.

Seeking medical help is essential if you think you or someone you know is suffering from depression.

Too many young people are lost to suicide each year in the UK, while friends and family were completely unaware of what their loved ones were going through.

Reaching out is never weak; it's the strongest thing you can do and can make a real difference.

Here is some information that *Mind Wise* have put together for anyone suffering with depression:

https://www.mindwisenv.org/mental-health-conditions/depression/

What is Anxiety?

Anxiety is another mental health problem, closely associated with depression. If someone suffers from one, it is likely they will suffer from the other as well. Anxiety symptoms can vary, involving both mental and physical symptoms, including:

- Uncontrollable worry and overthinking
- Difficulty concentrating
- Feelings of panic or of 'impending doom'
- Problems with falling or staying asleep
- Heavy and fast breathing, quickened heartbeat

If not treated, anxiety can trickle into different areas of your life and leave you feeling as though you are unable to cope with day-to-day tasks. Like with depression, consulting a doctor is of vital importance for people who think they may be struggling with anxiety.

Here is a link to some more information and support for people struggling with anxiety:

https://www.mindwisenv.org/mental-health-conditions/anxiety-disorders/

Coping with the pressure of financial goals

Saving can often be extremely difficult for young people. In today's age, goals that were once seen as normal, or "to be expected", such as getting out of the rent trap and buying your own house can sometimes seem like an unrealistic pipedream. In fact, saving for any big purchase can seem out of reach for a lot of young people.

Getting yourself down about the large purchases you feel you "should have" achieved by now is pointless, and it doesn't help you get there any quicker either. These "rite of passage" purchases - cars, house, weddings - are supposed to signify great leaps forward in life, but in the real world everyone does things at their own pace - there is no right or wrong way to live your life!

These things don't have to stress you. Setting realistic goals can lead to amazing results over the long term with a bit of self-discipline and focus. These don't even have to be long term commitments if you do it right.

Benefits to support you if you are struggling

As I mentioned earlier, in the Earn chapter, if you are in poor physical or mental health you may be entitled to Government benefits such as Employment Support Allowance and Personal Independence Payment.

Mental Health and Money Advice have put together a range of incredible resources that help make it very simple for anyone suffering with mental health issues to get access to any benefits they are entitled to.

This guide covers everything you need to know:

https://www.mentalhealthandmoneyadvice.org/en/welfare-benefits/can-i-claim-welfare-benefits-if-i-m-living-with-a-mental-illness/

TIPS FOR GETTING YOUR SAVINGS STARTED

Making Smart Purchases

Let's face it, we all make a lot of unnecessary purchases. Eating out, impulse buys, expensive holidays... But cutting back on the wasteful spending in your life can help your savings grow; these are short term cutbacks for long term benefit. According to *NimbleFins*, the average cost of a holiday per person in 2019 was £947. Adding £1,000 to your savings each year can make the goal of buying a house very realistic.

This doesn't mean you have to deny yourself all of life's pleasures - finding hobbies that you enjoy often don't require spending vast amounts of money and can give your life more meaning than the short-term rush of a new purchase or an overpriced getaway.

Additionally, as we touched upon in the Earn chapter, if you have a skill that you enjoy practising you may well be able to use this to earn some additional income while you are doing it!

Finding the Right Support

Support is all around us. Most of the time, we just don't know it. Finding the right support for you can be the difference between struggling every day and having a weight lifted off your shoulders. Deciding that you need help is not a weakness and it's nothing to be ashamed of - finding the right emotional and financial support to suit your needs is what's most important.

- Parents, Family and Friends - if you have people close to you, reach out to them for help. The people closest to you already know you, and will generally have your best interests at heart, so don't feel ashamed to turn to them and ask for help when you need it.
- Charity Support and Free Training - there are a range of charities right now that specialise in helping people learn to save and manage their money. Additionally, some banks and local community centres may offer training to help you get started on your financial journey.

Avoiding Con Artists

Ever heard of the term "Snake Oil Salesman"? It's an age-old nickname for someone who offers quick-fix cures, promising to make all your dreams come true and solve all of your problems.

That is until they turn out to be a crook who's sold you a potion of useless ingredients, taking the money of the needy, and fleeing to another town by the time anyone realises they've been conned. Just because it's an old turn of phrase doesn't mean we don't deal with these dodgy characters anymore – they've just mostly relocated to the world of cyberspace.

We've seen a major rise of these kinds of scams with the rise of email and social media – outrageous promises that they will "Change Your Life Forever", or that somebody wants to drop one million pounds into your bank account and all you need to do is fork over the details on your card. Just as you want to save, someone else wants to make a quick buck by cheating you out of your hard-earned money.

Be careful making deals on the internet – take the time to investigate the people and companies you invest time or money into and upskill on how to keep yourself safe online.

Not Falling for the "Too Good to be True"

Today on the internet, marketed "Get Rich Quick" schemes and pyramid schemes (or Multi-Level Marketing schemes, often abbreviated to MLMs) are everywhere.

These schemes thrive when the job market is slow, because this is when people have the most free time and are in need of easy money.

The idea is that you pay to buy into the scheme, recruit a number of people who in turn pay you, then each of those people recruit even more people, and money flows up the pyramid making everyone rich. That's what happens in theory. In the real world, the only people who make any money are those at the very top of the pyramid.

These schemes generally try to hide their underlying plan by saying that you are actually recruiting people to sell products (such as fitness shakes or expensive cosmetics) but the end result is the same: the people at the bottom lose all of their money. The bottom line to avoid falling victim to these schemes? Never put yourself in risk of exploitation or debt for the promise of a quick pay day, and always verify your sources. Websites such as GlassDoor and URLVoid can be used to quickly check the legitimacy of an opportunity or website, respectively, and there are many more similar sources on the web if you're ever in doubt.

MODERN ATTACKS ON OUR MENTAL HEALTH

COVID-19 and the Global Pandemic

The coronavirus pandemic has taken a heavy toll on many people's health and wellbeing. A combination of grieving, isolation, and the effects of economic recession have knocked many of us from our usual comfort zone and created a lot of hardship in people's lives. Between job losses, feelings of uncertainty, and loss of a social support network due to local lockdown restrictions, many of us were suddenly plunged into a world we were totally unfamiliar with. The following statistics give an insight into the effects of COVID on our mental health:

- 19.2% of adults in the UK experienced some form of depression during the coronavirus pandemic in June 2020; this is a significant increase from the numbers reported before the pandemic, with 9.7% recorded for the period July 2019 to March 2020.
- 12.9% of adults, so roughly one in eight people, developed moderate to severe symptoms of depression during the coronavirus pandemic, with a further 6.2% going on to experience this level of symptoms long-term.

- Feelings of stress and anxiety were the most reported way that adults experiencing depression felt their well-being was being affected, with 84.9% stating this as their primary cause for concern during the pandemic.

Effects of Social Media

In terms of technological innovation, platforms such as Facebook and Instagram are fantastic tools; they allow for instant long-range communication, and the chance to reach out to others - potentially even the entire world. But is it really all positive out there?

Despite the "social" aspect of social media, using these platforms do not always have the impact you'd expect.

In 2018, The University of Pennsylvania carried out a study into the use of Facebook, Snapchat, and Instagram, and concluded that "Using less social media than you normally would leads to significant decreases in both depression and loneliness."

Additionally, there are many "influencers" out there trying to exploit people with their seemingly perfect lifestyles and the paid advertising that goes with them.

There are two dangerous aspects to this ploy - not only are people exposed to predatory and often misleading adverts, but they are also being shamed for not being as "successful" as the airbrushed personalities they see online.

Trying to measure up against these impossible standards and being told that you can only meet them by buying this moisturizer, or this diet tea, can end up really hurting your self-esteem – not to mention your bank balance!

Targeted Advertising

Digital marketing is a sector which has exploded in recent years.

Generally, this involves a scheme by which people's information feeds are deliberately manipulated, so that a given advert is shown to people who are most likely to interact with them. Say for example you search online for a particular brand of shoes; you're then added to a database of people who are likely to buy this kind of shoe. Soon it will start to feel like advertisements for shoes are following you all over the internet – and that's because they are.

This phenomenon doesn't end at the search bar either; if you have a smart control hub in your home, you're likely handing your data over to advertisers every single day.

It's fair to say that this practice does have some positives – as the algorithm begins to learn what you want, it may well suggest some great items personalised for you, cutting down on time spent browsing. But of course, there is a more dangerous side to targeted advertising, as it can end up having one of two effects on our mental health:

- Make us more aware that we can't always afford the things we want, which can lead to us feeling inadequate.
- Trigger us to make impulsive purchases that push us into debt, setting you back further in your finance journey possibly before you've even begun.

Gambling

Gambling has become a massive problem amongst young people in the UK in recent times and can be very harmful if it gets out of control.

I have dedicated an entire chapter in this book to gambling, including information there about how to spot the signs of problem gambling and what to do if you feel gambling is becoming an issue for you.

If you or someone you know is struggling with a gambling addiction, contact the National Gambling Helpline for free on 0808 8020 133. Their phone line is completely non-judgemental and confidential.

In-Game Purchases

Whether you're a lifelong gamer or just like to de-stress with a short burst of Candy Crush, something to watch out for is in-game purchases.

The sounds and visuals that are used in "loot box" scenes are very similar to that of a casino arcade's slot machines, and this is an intentional design.

The creators of these applications use exciting and bright visuals to trigger a response in the gamers that encourages them to spend more and more.

This can be especially painful with mobile phone app games. As these are generally very simple and innocuous in nature, they aren't as immediately alarming as say a game played in a casino or a bet placed in a bookmaker's shop.

We don't register them as gambling at all. But we can fall into traps of buying more and more upgrades or features. We start to gamble and invest money into the games which can lead to very harmful debt without us even realising.

HOW CAN I OVERCOME STRESS AND MANAGE MY MENTAL HEALTH?

There are a few techniques which can be very effective for combating stress and helping you avoid negative thought cycles. For serious mental health issues, your GP should always be consulted and kept informed on your mental health progress, however for day-to-day mental health maintenance it can be helpful to keep practicing the following behaviours.

Don't Be So Hard on Yourself

This is the most important thing to remember - sometimes we all make mistakes. We make bad choices and spend beyond our budgets, it happens. It can be extremely stressful, especially if your budget is tight. You should be trying to stick to your budgets and not overspend on things that aren't necessary, but sometimes this happens, and you can't treat yourself like public enemy number one for a small slip in your judgement. Take responsibility but do not let a small mistake change how you feel about yourself. Tomorrow is another day!

Practicing Mindfulness

This is a practice similar to Buddhist thought - you focus on thinking about your thinking.

By focusing on our thinking, we can calm anxieties and become more aware of our thoughts.

Using meditation techniques, we learn to identify our feelings and what thoughts are causing them in the first place.

We can use mindfulness to meditate and centre ourselves in the present moment, rather than getting lost in worry. In the long term, we can begin to actually replace those feelings as well. Research this practice online and see can it work for you!

Personal Development

Like looking after your body's health with exercise and diet, it's well worth dedicating time towards looking after your mental health.

There are plenty of books that you can read to help you develop good reflexes for dealing with stress and it's worth putting that time into arming yourself so that you are ready to face any situation.

A book I would recommend for when you're starting out on this journey of self-development is "How to Keep Calm and Carry On; Inspiring Ways to Worry Less and Live a Happier Life" by Professor Daniel Freeman and published by Pearson Books.

ASK YOURSELF: WHAT'S THE WORST-CASE SCENARIO?

Even if you are in a lot of debt, the government in the United Kingdom offers many strategies to help. If you are at the stage where your debts are unmanageable and cannot be repaid with traditional repayment plans, you have two main choices:

- Declare **bankruptcy.**
- Take out an **IVA (Individual Voluntary Agreement)**

Neither of these options are particularly attractive to most people if they can avoid them. But they are actionable next steps that we can take if we've tried everything else.

Declaring Bankruptcy

Bankruptcy is a scary word. Most people have no idea how it works, but when you break it down it's actually not that scary. There is negative social stigma surrounding bankruptcy and it can affect your lifestyle and possibly future career prospects in some cases.

If you cannot pay your debts, you can apply for bankruptcy. This is a 12-month process where your debt is put aside and you have certain restrictions placed upon you. The debt is not completely written off - your assets will be seized to pay off the debts as much as is possible.

The British Government places restrictions on bankrupt individuals. They are not allowed to:

- Borrow over £500 without declaring that they are bankrupt.
- Work as an insolvency practitioner (someone specialising in debt).
- Work in 'high up' corporate roles, such as director, manager, or promoter.

You will also be signed up to the **Individual Insolvency Register.** This is a searchable database for people who want to find out about any past bankruptcies and other debt-related issues a potential client might have (such as banks or private lenders).

Bankruptcy isn't something to enter into lightly and should be avoided if you can help it. It means that you will struggle to get loans in the future, including mortgages. But it will relieve the short-term pressure of loans and means you can begin to rebuild your credit score.

IVA

An IVA or Individual Voluntary Agreement is an agreement to pay back creditors over a defined period of time. It could be expensive so before making any decisions take advice from a qualified Insolvency Practitioner.

An IVA may be preferable to bankruptcy if you:

- own a home, or other assets, that you don't want to lose

- own your own business
- may lose your job if you go bankrupt, for example, if you are a police officer or work in the armed forces
- have, or are considering applying for, a power of attorney on behalf of someone
- have some spare income each month or a lump sum of money to make repayments to creditors
- want to avoid the negative stigma of bankruptcy

Debt Charities: StepChange

StepChange is a debt charity operating in the United Kingdom. It aims to help people get out of debt with free advice. They can facilitate bankruptcy declarations as well as plan effective debt plans to help someone plan their way out.

Getting out of debt can be a difficult and terrifying experience for many people. Especially if you have no financial training or your debts are very large. *StepChange* offers solutions to problems, supports the people who ring them for as long as is necessary, and actively fights for better ways to treat "problem debt".

Before considering declaring bankruptcy, you should absolutely contact *StepChange*. They are dedicated professionals who work very hard to help people in perilous debt. Your individual needs will be addressed with their range of plans that can help you the most.

Who Else Can I Turn To?

If you're in a crisis and need someone to talk to, the *Samaritans* are always there. Founded in 1953, they have made it their business to help people who need to reach out.

"In an emergency, the citizen turns to the telephone and dials 999. There ought to be an emergency number for suicidal people, I thought".

Those are the words of Chad Varah, the man who founded the *Samaritans*. His aim is still true today. Mental health crises that lead to suicide attempts are medical emergencies. Having someone to talk to can make all the difference.

If you are at risk of a mental health crisis, you can contact the Samaritans on 116123.

Lifeline also offer support to people experiencing despair and can be contacted on 0808 808 8000.

If you are under 19, you can also speak to Childline confidentially about any issue you are upset about for free at any time of the day or night on 0800 1111.

Mental Health and Money Toolkit

The Mental Health and Money Charity were set up to help you understand, manage and improve your mental health and resolve any money issues.

They have put together a toolkit to help you manage, improve and manage your mental and financial health. Please check it out using the link below as it really is a great tool:

https://www.mentalhealthandmoneyadvice.org/en/toolkit

The Bottom Line

When you're struggling with money, and especially when you are encountering mental health struggles on top of this, it can sometimes feel like you have nowhere to turn. This is absolutely not the case. If you can, reach out to your friends and family - they may not be trained professionals, but they will want to know if you are in hard times and may be able to provide emotional support.

Additionally, it is imperative that you reach out for help from the professionals, whether this be your local GP, the Samaritans, or a specially trained therapist or counsellor in your area, although the private therapy route can be costly.

If you have never experienced mental health issues before, reaching out in the first place can often be the most daunting part of the recovery process. But you are not alone, and you are not the first person to have felt this way. You deserve to get better.

Chapter 7

The Rise of Casual Gambling

Since the United Kingdom's regulations on gambling were made more lenient in 2005, and with mobile phones becoming an essential item, the rise of casual gambling in recent years has been astounding. In the past to place a bet you had to go to a bookies shop which was an intimidating place filled mostly with older men smoking and watching horse racing, but now it's much more accessible and can be done from the comfort of your own home.

From the High Street to Your Pocket

When I was young, the only way you could bet was to visit a bookmaker's shop, where you would be asked for ID and turned away if you were found to be under 18. These days all you need to do is reach into your pocket and you can bet on anything you like: bingo, online casinos, football, UFC, the options are pretty much endless.

What's more, friendly celebrity faces you know and trust are paid by gambling companies to entice you to visit colourful friendly sites and apps, to place bets and potentially win some big money. The attraction is obvious. You could turn a bit of spare change into a fortune in a few minutes!

The Law on Gambling

It is illegal for anyone under the age of 18 to place a bet or even enter a bookmaker's shop. In addition, as of April 2021, the minimum age for participation in the National Lottery has moved from 16 to 18.

Society's View on Gambling

In some cultures, gambling is completely banned due to religious reasons or simply because of the problems it causes in society. In many countries where it is outlawed, gambling is still operated by shady black-market bookmakers often controlled by organised crime gangs, but in the UK, it is legal and often accepted as a fairly harmless vice. Most people in the UK see putting a pound or two on a horse during the Grand National as a harmless bit of fun.

"The Bookie Always Wins"

This is an old saying about the perils of gambling. Gaming companies make an obscene amount of profit. Getting the bookies off the high street and into people's pockets has been extremely good business for these companies.

They will employ experts who can understand the odds in meticulous detail and are able to set them in such a way that it is enough for some people to win occasionally, meaning you don't feel short changed as you see it can be done once in a blue moon.

Once people feel this excitement when they win some money, gambling can quickly become addictive.

According to a BBC news report in April 2021, the boss of one of the biggest gambling companies in the UK paid herself one of the biggest salaries in UK corporate history in 2020/2021. Her salary was a mind boggling 421 million pounds for that tax year.

While I make no personal judgement on her or how she chooses to make her money, this fact simply demonstrates the point that these companies put a lot of energy into ensuring that most gamblers lose, so that they can turn a more handsome profit for themselves.

Gambling and Young People

Despite the law prohibiting young people from gambling, in recent times problem gambling has still made its way into the lives of today's young people. There are a number of potential reasons for this; possibly due to the boredom of lockdown in 2020 or the resulting increased unemployment among young adults. Ultimately, for many it seems like a way to inject some excitement into their days. The rise in popularity of gambling is often linked to adverts on TV encouraging people to take risks for fun and the abundance of online information about gambling, including social media accounts offering tips and information about where to find the best odds.

Despite many gambling companies setting up safeguards ensuring people who register on their sites verify their age when they subscribe, there is still a startling rise in the number of young people taking part in these activities.

According to the Young People and Gambling Survey, conducted in 2020 by Ipsos MORI on behalf of the Gambling Commission, 37% of 11 to 16 year olds in England and Scotland have gambled in the last 12 months. This is a very worrying statistic because, aside from being illegal, it is also concerning to know that many young people are getting into habits that could become very harmful to them now and in later life.

"Once the Fun Stops, Stop"

This catchy phrase is the disclaimer all bookies use to discourage people from losing money they can't afford. The ironic thing about this is that for many people it only stops being fun once you have lost more than you can afford to lose, by which time it is far too late.

Gambling is the last of the great vices that are still allowed to advertise on daytime television. Smoking, alcohol and fried food have all been banned, however children and adults are still bombarded with advertisements during their favourite games and shows, with ads encouraging them to "spend to win". Bingo, loot boxes, betting on football... These are all forms of gambling regardless of their modern form, with their exciting graphics, fun friend-making opportunities, and with guaranteed pay-outs.

PROBLEM GAMBLING

Gambling can be very harmful as it often preys on those in society who are most at risk of becoming addicted in the first place.

Problem gambling works much the same as any other addiction, where the addicted person needs more and more of the stimulation to keep getting the same "hit". In this case, the stimulation is the adrenaline that comes from taking a risk to be in with a chance of securing a big payoff.

The gambling industry deliberately markets this behaviour as a fun and harmless pastime, but if allowed to become a habit this can become very dangerous and land you in a lot of debt. As we looked at in previous chapters, debt can lead to all sorts of mental health issues.

A report commissioned by the House of Lords called "Gambling Harm – Time For Action" states that over 300 suicides a year in the UK are as a result of gambling addiction, and The Gambling Commission stated in 2020 that approximately 55,000 young people aged 11 to 16 across England, Scotland and Wales were classified as problem gamblers.

How can I tell if I have a problem with gambling?

Here are some (but not all) of the tell-tale signs according to *GamCare* (an amazing organisation who offer help to people struggling with problem gambling):

- Do you find yourself spending more than you had set out to?
- Are you spending significant periods of time gambling?
- Do you ever find yourself concealing your behaviour or lying about your actions when it comes to betting?
- Is gambling affecting your relationships with family or friends?
- Is gambling affecting your school, university or work?

If the answer to any of these is yes, and gambling is getting in the way of you living the life you want to live, then it might be worth considering taking some action to reduce your gambling or consider stopping altogether.

What can I do if I think I might have a gambling issue?

If you have a feeling that you are not in control or it is having a negative effect on your life, trust your gut. It may be the case that it hasn't fully dawned on you that it is affecting you negatively. It is often something that people feel ashamed to discuss and therefore all you see from the various WhatsApp groups you're in is about who got a big win or what your friends think might be the next hot tip.

No one would want to brag about spending their rent money on a bet they didn't win to try and regain losses they made on a previous binge, or the debt they're landing their families in. This less glamorous side of gabling isn't talked about with as much enthusiasm for obvious reasons.

If you are worried about your gambling or the gambling of someone close to you, reach out.

Log on to https://www.bigdeal.org.uk/ to live chat with a *GamCare* adviser 24 hours day.

alternatively you can reach out to *Gamcare* via email at YoungPeopleService@gamcare.com or via phone by calling 020 3902 6964.

If you find out that you do need a bit of support you will find lots of useful information and advice on the https://www.bigdeal.org.uk/ site, including self-help plans, and non-judgmental support services designed to help people recovering from gambling addiction.

There are also organisations like The *National Gambling Helpline* who can provide guidance to young people, as well as parents, carers, and others who may be concerned about a young person's gambling. They can be contacted by freephone 0808 80 20 133, 24 hours a day, every day of the year.

First Steps to Break the Habit

There are practical steps you can take like self-excluding yourself from gambling sites and venues if you feel that this would help.

Most gambling companies and venues offer this service.

You could consider restricting your access to money (ask someone you trust to handle your cash while you sort out any issues you might have), and some banks such as Monzo also offer this service to restrict your spending. However, seeking professional advice is definitely the best way to start your journey.

If you or someone you know is struggling with a gambling addiction, contact the National Gambling Helpline for free on 0808 8020 133. Their phone line is completely non-judgmental and confidential. You can visit www.bigdeal.org.uk and www.gamcare.org.uk for more information and excellent resources.

Chapter 8
Property: Renting vs Buying

Leaving home and making your first steps as a free adult is liberating. Whether you are living in a rented property or are fortunate enough to buy somewhere straight away, getting your own place is a rite of passage for many. Owning a house features on the list of long-term goals for most young people, especially in the United Kingdom.

In other European countries home ownership is not such a big deal, with rent-controlled housing and a bigger stock of public houses meaning that it isn't as sought after a life goal. However, because there has been such a rise in property values, so much money to be made from renting out property and such a lack of public housing here, many parents tell their children that it is very important to get "on the property ladder" as soon as possible.

Many older people in the UK are now "property rich" and "cash poor".

House prices have increased massively over the last 50 years. For many older people in the UK, their houses will be their main source of income in retirement rather than their pensions.

Many of the "boomer" generation may have been lucky to buy a house quite easily, earlier in life than young people could expect to do nowadays.

These houses may well have risen extremely sharply over the years as well, leaving the homeowners sitting on properties that are now worth a lot of money.

Many plan to downsize or use an equity release plan and use the money they will "release" from the value of their homes to help provide their income in retirement.

Why it's important to think about home ownership early

Workplace pension plans used to be a lot more generous, with many historically offering an income for life based on the length of time served in the job and the final salary the member had when they left the business.

These old-style pensions have become so expensive for companies to run (what with people living longer) that most private companies now choose to offer a much more slimmed down, cheaper version which isn't as expensive to operate and puts the responsibility onto the saver to be proactive to save up more.

The more modern pension provides something more like a savings pot and the ability to access the money flexibly means that many people will run out of money before they run out of life.

When we keep this in mind, alongside the increasing house prices and the competitive job market for young people, the sooner you can get a house to live in and have it paid off the easier it will be to purchase other assets that will provide an income in later life e.g. paying into pension schemes or investments

Pros and cons of renting and buying

In this chapter we will consider the benefits of having your own home, and the things you need to take into consideration when looking at renting or buying a property.

Breaking down the pros and cons of renting and buying is important for helping you make these big life decisions.

A rental agreement might only last a year, but a bad reference from a landlord can follow you around. A bad mortgage could be with you for over 35 years - that's almost half the average life expectancy!

RENTING

How do you get a good deal renting?

Renting can be tough on bank accounts.

Since 2009, rent prices have consistently grown at an alarming rate. If you're not careful, you can end up paying more money in rent than you should be, making it difficult to budget for any other goals.

Finding a good house is only half the battle - you need to find a good landlord too.

A good landlord can be judged as one who sets a fair rent, works to keep your house in good repair, and is willing to help you when you need support. There are services such as The Tenant's Voice which help renters find good (and bad) landlords so that you can make the most informed choice.

What do I need to know about renting?

Depending on who your landlord is, your renting experience can be very different.

Reports of horror landlords who don't respect their tenants and cause a great deal of stress aren't uncommon. Although nothing guarantees a good time in a rented property, here's a checklist of things you must have to protect you legally:

- A rental agreement or lease (either fixed term or periodic, e.g. month to month)
- A deposit or alternative payment that offers you protection (like house insurance)
- An inventory of goods in the residence

These three things can protect your rights should you need to. Additionally, the landlord should also provide you with a copy of the "How to Rent Guide" if you are renting in England and a Tenant Information Pack if you rent in Scotland. Know your rights, know your responsibilities, and know your landlord's responsibilities.

Are all rental homes the same?

No - depending on your circumstances you might be able to get council housing (or public renting). This means that you pay the local council for your housing. There is a huge demand for public housing right now in England. Over 1 million people were on the waiting list to be housed in 2020, and an expectation that this will double in 2021. If you want one, you might have to wait a long time.

On the other hand, you can work with a private landlord. This means that they own the house outright and rent it to you without government involvement. These set-ups can be found commonly throughout the country but shop around to find the best deal.

There's a lot of variation out there, and that's just in the kind of landlord. Renting allows you to live in as small or as big a property as you need. If you only need a small amount of space and want to save up, a bedsit (bedroom, living space, and kitchen combined) might be perfect. Flats, small houses, and even large homes the size of mansions can be rented out to people who can afford them.

What kind of rental agreements are there?

All agreements can be split into two groups - fixed term or periodic. Neither one of them is better than the other, but you should think about your needs and how long you intend to stay in one place before committing.

Fixed term

A fixed term agreement has a specific amount of time clearly stated within the contract that the tenant can use the house. Commonly, these are listed as 6 month or 1-year leases, but they can extend for any amount of time. Sometimes these contracts become periodic agreements after the end of the fixed term.

These are better for people who know they will be settling in an area for a set amount of time.

Although you can break the agreement, sometimes this incurs penalties or surrendering the deposit.

Periodic

As opposed to the long-term agreement of a fixed term contract, periodic contracts "rollover" a certain period. Month to month contracts are common, but week to week and even year to year contracts are not unheard of.

These contracts are perfect for people who have to move around a lot. The shorter lease means that they don't need to worry about charges for breaking the contract earlier, but they are less secure as they require renewing regularly.

KNOW YOUR RIGHTS

Knowing your rights as a renter is important, so read about and make sure potential landlords know that you understand your rights.

There are several landlords out there who might use shady practices to make as much money as possible, so understanding how the law supports you is key.

Five tips for getting the best deal when you are renting:

Tip 1. Don't Pay Unnecessary Fees

Since June 2020, it has been illegal for landlords to charge "tenancy related fees". These include fees for checking references, credit checks, and renewing a contract.

This is actually a very serious crime on the landlord's side.

Repeat offenders can be prosecuted and even banned from being a landlord in the future. I

f you feel a landlord has tried to charge you for a tenancy fee, get in touch with trading standards and letting agent redress schemes. Having the correct support to deal with dodgy dealers is key.

Tip 2. Make Sure the House Is Safe

Before moving in, you should check out the house and make sure that everything is in order. If you sign a contract and find out conditions are not suitable, you will still be on the hook for rent payments (without even living there!).

Safe doesn't just mean no exposed electrical wires.

All rental properties should have a smoke alarm on each floor, carbon monoxide detectors near danger spots (boilers, coal fires, etc.), a gas safety certificate, Portable Appliance Testing (PAT) approval for electronic equipment, fire-resistant furniture, and a functioning water supply.

If you find that the house does not have these, don't sign a contract and report your findings.

Just because you've spotted a danger doesn't mean someone else will.

Tip 3. Note Any Damages When You Move In

When you sign for a house, you will be given an inventory. This will lay out clearly all ongoing work to the house and any damage from previous tenants. Taking pictures or recording videos of any damages you find in your new home is crucial for building evidence.

Landlords (rightly or wrongly) have a reputation for claiming entire deposits even when there is no need for compensation.

If you have picture evidence proving your innocence, claiming your deposit back for damages that are wrongly attributed to you can make life a lot easier.

Tip 4. Make Sure Your Deposit Is Protected

Because your deposit is in a bit of a "no man's land" during your tenancy, there are government schemes set up to help you make sure you get back what you put in. Your landlord is legally obliged to make sure they protect your deposit as well if you have an assured shorthold tenancy - it's not just free money for them.

From the date the deposit is received, a landlord has 30 days to protect your deposit with one of three protection scheme providers and provide you written proof. There isn't a great deal of difference between the protection services - the only important thing is that your money is with one of them!

The three major services:

- *Deposit Protection Service (DPS)*
- *Tenancy Deposit Scheme (TDS)*
- *Mydeposits*

If your landlord fails to do so, you can claim compensation up to 6 years after the event. Also, you gain some protections against eviction - you can't be served a Section 21 eviction notice if there is no deposit protection scheme in place.

5. Tell Your Landlord When You Need Repairs

Things break, houses get worn, and sometimes they need to be repaired. That's fine. Your landlord is generally responsible for maintaining the outside of the house. You are responsible for maintaining the inside of the rented space, but you are not expected to be able to fix every problem.

If you need a repair done which you cannot do yourself, tell them as soon as you can. This stops the job from growing into something more unmanageable and helps you get your house back in working order as soon as possible. These costs should be covered by the landlord unless there is reason to believe you broke your tenancy agreement.

For some jobs, you are not legally allowed to attempt repairs (unless you have the correct qualifications, but even then, it's best to check with the landlord).

The most obvious example is the boiler - if you are not a registered technician, it is against the law to try and repair it yourself. You shouldn't do any more than restarting it if it cuts out. Learn what you are allowed to repair and what you should get help with!

WHAT'S THE BEST WAY TO SAVE FOR A DEPOSIT?

When we looked at **Investing** we discussed the different options available and the "volatility" of different types of investments. The type of investment you should use depends on the amount of time you are planning to keep the money invested. We saw that the best returns might be made from higher risk investment types.

Stocks and shares can increase in a very impressive way. We also looked at Stocks and Shares ISAs in the Investing section, as a tax efficient way of raising money for long-term goals.

As an example: the American Stock Market Index, the S&P 500, has grown by an average of around 10% every year since it started up in 1926, however stocks and shares run in cycles and so can drop by up to 30% in a bad year and can take a long time to recover.

Therefore, having all your savings in this type of investment could throw you away off track if the market crashed the year before you had planned to buy your first home.

Using some type of savings account that gives a decent return, and that will not drop if the markets crash, would probably be the most suitable for most people. When we were looking at savings accounts, you will probably remember that most savings accounts don't produce much return or interest at all currently. There is one product that has been set up by the government to help young people get on the property ladder.

What Is A Lifetime ISA?

When saving to buy a home, you can open a Lifetime Individual Savings Account (LISA) designed to help those saving for later life or first-time buyer homes. The account works by giving the prospective buyer a 25% on whatever they managed to save over that year.

We cover this product in detail in the Saving chapter.

What do I need to know before opening A Lifetime ISA if I plan to buy a house?

Remember that there are a few conditions:

- The property must cost less than £450,000.

- Your Lifetime ISA must have been open for at least 12 months at the time of purchase.
- The payment goes directly through a conveyancer or a solicitor - the money does not sit in your account.
- You must buy a property with a mortgage - you cannot buy one outright.

If you can fulfil all those criteria, the Lifetime ISA scheme is an excellent way to get 25% extra on your savings for buying that first house. Although they are not set up with only renters in mind, they are very powerful tools for shrewd renters who want to put money away over many years.

BUYING

How do I get a good deal buying?

Buying a home is a huge task which requires you to go out and look for the house that you want to buy. Being happy with your property is important as you are the one who is responsible for it - even if you have a mortgage, you are the one paying for the repairs and maintenance.

So, we know that we are responsible for the house completely. But that just means that there are potentially high costs for owning, so why would anyone do it?

Why should I want to buy a house?

Owning a home is probably the most "adult" thing you can do. It's a sign of healthy finances, the ability to manage a household and shows a level of responsibility. Along with getting married and potentially starting a family, it is high up on the list of priorities for many.

More than that, owning a house means escaping the rent trap.

Renting can lead to many years of financially treading water - you earn money to pay your landlord, but don't gain anything for it personally. You are paying off your landlord's mortgage, and the entire time the property may well be gaining in value – something that your landlord will benefit from. Paying off a mortgage adds value to your home in equity.

As you pay more into your mortgage, your payments are added to the value of the home. This raises the value of your investment as well as giving you a valuable source of cash if you need to release equity. Once you start paying off a mortgage, you are investing into an asset.

Assets in this case mean anything which you own. A house is an asset and probably the most expensive asset you will ever own. As you pay off a mortgage and eventually own the house outright, you will constantly be investing in your own portfolio and increase your own personal net worth.

What is a Mortgage?

A mortgage is a special kind of long-term loan - coming from the French for "death pledge", it is a loan that will last for most of your life. As they are for very large sums of money, mortgages are mainly for purchasing houses.

Not all mortgages are made equal, however. Depending on your income, you will need to offer a percentage of the total loan. This can be between 5% and 30% usually.

Although it can be attractive just to get any mortgage, the lower the deposit, the higher the interest. The more money you can contribute as a down-payment, the less you will have to pay off later down the line.

How much should I expect to pay for a mortgage?

Let's say you want to buy a house worth £250,000 and you need a mortgage to cover most of that cost. If you are applying for a first time buyer mortgage, you may be able to get a mortgage to cover 95% of the cost through a government scheme (These have other conditions attached so speak to a mortgage adviser to see if this is suitable). These offers aren't always available, so we'll use 90% as our example.

First, we need to work out the deposit:

£250,000 ÷ 10 = £25,000

A mortgage for a £250,000 house would need a 10% deposit of £25,000. This is still a huge amount of money, so saving up should become a priority as soon as you can if you are planning to own a home.

Your mortgage repayments are worked out concerning the cost of your total mortgage debt. This depends on the mortgage amount, the rate of interest, and the length of the mortgage. Using our £250,000 example, we'll say the interest rate is 3% and our mortgage lasts for 25 years.

Over 35 years, you have 420 months to pay back the debt. Your total repayment should total around £865.91 per month, along with £562.50 in interest (set at 3% of the total debt). This is a huge cost, so make sure that you are financially able to shoulder it. Remember that the interest rate can change depending on the type of product you use so make sure you would still be able to afford the payments if they increased by 3% for example.

Due to interest, you will be paying more than the initial size of the mortgage over its lifespan.

The exact amount can change, so be sure to regularly check up on the interest rate and if you can find good deals or tricks to bring that number down.

When can I get a mortgage?

Banks don't tend to give a minimum (or maximum) age for mortgages outright, but they do give a checklist of qualities that they expect from a mortgage applicant. They need to know:

1. How much you earn

Ideally, your income should be steady for at least 6 months prior to applying for a mortgage and give you enough money to cover the monthly repayments. This is a lot easier for people who are not self-employed, so if you are working as an artist or contractor you will need to gather more proof of previous and future earnings.

When applying for a mortgage, you're kind of going to an audition. The lender wants to know that they can trust you with their money and that they will get something back from their "investment" in you. You will need to show that you can afford repayments and are responsible with money.

This includes bank statements over the long term. For people in conventional employment, this could be 3 months' worth.

For the self-employed, this could be up to 3 years of full financial reports (including tax information) to show that you have consistent cash flow and are capable of such a large commitment.

2. Proof of Identity

Before they can grant you a mortgage, you need to prove who you are. A passport or driving license is fine for showing who you are, but you also need to show that you have a bank account that has a steady cash flow.

3. Your Credit History

What's a credit rating? In short, it's a rating you receive on how well you pay back your debts.

If you have never taken on debt (or credit) before, you won't have a credit rating. If a loan manager can't see a credit history, they don't know if you are good with money.

You can find more information on Credit Files in the Borrowing section.

4. Tenants on the mortgage

It is possible to get a mortgage if you are a sole buyer, but it is more difficult. Generally, you won't be able to get as big a mortgage as applicants in a couple or a group of friends moving in together.

Finding people to move in with can increase the size of the mortgage you can receive, but it does mean having a long-term debt between multiple people.

Before buying with friends or as a young couple, discuss what should happen if you need to go your separate ways.

5. Value of the Property

You can't get a mortgage if you don't know what you want to buy. Discussing your plans with a loan manager will help you figure out the best plans for the house you want to buy. Expensive houses will need expensive mortgages, so consider how much you can realistically pay each month.

Before actually receiving the mortgage to pay for the house, you will receive the mortgage in principle - this means that the loan will be approved when you put the offer in for the house.

What Is "The Property Ladder" I hear people banging on about?

"Getting on the property ladder" means buying a house and making your first step as a homeowner.

Because the barrier to entering the housing market is so high (many people simply can't afford to save up for a mortgage), actually getting onto the ladder is far harder than "climbing" it to better properties.

If you can get a property at a young age, you have managed to do the hard work early on in your life.

Now you can focus on paying off your mortgage and probably get to retirement age with a lot less to worry about.

That's not to say getting on the ladder later can ruin plans for retirement, but it certainly makes it easier to make it off earlier.

When do people usually buy their first homes?

The average age for first time buyers in the UK has been getting higher steadily over the years.

While some older people might have been able to buy a small house as a teenager, today it is extremely difficult without help from someone else such as a parent or a partner.

The average age for first time buyers in 2020 was 34 years old, which is a massive increase of 21% since 2007 before the financial crash, when the average age was 28. This shows us clearly that people are finding it more and more difficult to get onto the property ladder.

Getting onto the property ladder earlier allows you more time to make changes to your investment - you can upgrade, build equity, and develop your investment.

If you are particularly successful, building a portfolio of houses might be possible providing you with passive income in later life.

What is the average price for buying a home?

The average price nationwide was £262,175 in 2020, but this greatly differs across the country. People living in London were paying on average £490,936 for a new home, which is more than three times the £136,281 a prospective buyer would have to pay in the North East.

Finding the right home for you can be difficult. It is a huge financial commitment over more than 20 years, so finding the home that you want that fits into your budget can be a stressful experience.

What happens if I can't keep paying my mortgage?

If you can't keep up your mortgage payments, the lender can claim back what they are owed.

This is almost always the house, meaning that you are left with a bad credit score, no house, and no equity. In short, failing to pay a mortgage leads to pretty serious consequences.

If you find yourself falling behind, contact a debt charity like *StepChange* for help working out how to approach your debt. Their number is 0800 138 11 11.

Do not bury your head in the sand. Be upfront and speak to your lender to discuss a payment plan, explain what you can afford and see how they can help.

Some providers can even offer short payment holidays for clients in financial difficulties. Some borrowers may even give you the option to reduce the payments down so that you only pay the interest for a while and leave the capital outstanding until you can start paying again.

How can getting on the property ladder help my mental health?

Hopefully, you've seen that owning a property can lead to a lot of positives for the long term. Most of all, the importance of knowing that you are investing in your own future can be a huge positive for young buyers.

If you have set up your mortgage correctly, you can expect to have the entire debt paid by the time you approach retirement. This means that you no longer have to worry about large, monthly payments and can use the value that is tied up in your house to support whatever you want to do in later life.

The cost of renting varies across the country, but let's say that you pay £800 per month for our rent. Over a year, that's £9,600 put into someone else's pocket. (Probably paying off someone else's mortgage). The ability to invest that in your own property is a huge bonus that grows every year and can be used later on for drawing on this equity and reinvesting.

Living at home as a way to save

Depending on your needs at any particular time in your life, if you don't mind living at home this can be a useful time to put money aside. If you need your own space, renting might actually be the best solution for you while you sort out other priorities like completing education. But for most people, getting onto the property ladder sooner rather than later and investing in your future is the best option.

Saving up enough money to get a deposit is the most difficult step for prospective first-time buyers, but using government backed schemes and saving wisely can give you the best outcome possible. You need to think carefully about how you approach your spending as well - banks want to know if you are good with money or if you spend it as soon as you have it.

Speak to a Mortgage Adviser

Consult expert advice from a well-reviewed mortgage adviser before taking out a mortgage and get them to explain about the different products available to you, as well as explaining the pros and cons of each one before you make a decision on what mortgage product would suit your needs best.

Ask lots of questions! Additionally, while you are saving, spending some time learning about the market in your area will give you a head start in getting onto the ladder, escaping the rent trap, and making one of the most rewarding investment decisions of your life.

Chapter 9

Keeping Yourself Financially Healthy

Maintaining your financial health is just like looking after your body's health. If you want to keep your body healthy you will get yourself into good habits, eating healthy food and exercising regularly.

Once you master these basics you may be able to avoid common preventable illnesses such as type 2 diabetes or obesity.

To a certain extent your financial health can be maintained by following many of the tips in this guide, becoming fluent in the language of finance, and developing a healthy relationship with money.

Some societies find it a bit taboo talking about money and wealth, as it could be perceived as being greedy or stingy or whatever.

It's nothing to be ashamed of or be scared of as it is unfortunately something we all need to get to grips with if we are to live well in a modern society.

Setting goals, then checking in regularly to see how your plans are developing will become second nature.

Keep Yourself Educated

There are so many resources out there to keep you up to speed with what is going on in the world of finance.

The *Money Charity and Money Advice Service* (soon to be known as the Money and Pension Service) offer free support so you never need to go uninformed.

The earlier you put a plan together the better because who knows what society will look like when you reach old age. People are living longer and the public purse is becoming more and more stretched, so this generation might find themselves having to fend for themselves more than previous generations later on in life.

Seek Professional Advice

Getting a good financial planner to help you once you feel ready is a very useful thing to have.

Make sure you only work with advisers who are regulated by the Financial Conduct Authority, the government's financial watchdog.

You can find local advisers who are highly rated on www.unbiased.co.uk.

Always be sure to ask about all charges that will be payable and ask them to demonstrate why these charges represent good value for money.

Take A Step Back Every So Often

Sometimes we find ourselves getting so wrapped up in the things we're doing, that we begin to lose sight as to why we are doing them. It's useful to occasionally earmark some time away from your usual routine to reflect on things that are going on in your life.

Ask yourself why you do the things you do. What are your end goals? What makes you happy?

Are you studying something or working somewhere because you thought it was what was expected of you by others?

When you work out a good work/life balance and are able to earn enough money to live happily you are winning. It's never too late to change direction or try new things.

Don't let short term setbacks discourage you.

There will always be things that happen to you that you hadn't planned for.

Businesses may go under. The economy might crash. You might get ill and have to spend all your savings. This is the nature of life. If you look at any successful wealthy person, it is almost inevitable that they will have experienced minor and perhaps major setbacks on the road to where they are now.

Donald Trump (who heralds himself as a very successful person) owned six businesses that had to file for bankruptcy between 1991 and 2009 yet he still went on to become the President of the United States and amass a fortune of several billion dollars.

For the record, please trust me, I'm not using "The Donald" as a role model by any means, but I think it demonstrates the point that the path to success is not always straightforward.

A Goal Without a Plan is Just a Wish

When you work out what you want to do in years to come or decide where you want to be by a certain age, make sure you do something about it.

Keep yourself accountable at regular intervals. Be it annually or however often you feel is necessary.

Whether it is just educating yourself in a particular field or saving towards a particular goal as long as you are making tangible progress, you're doing it right.

Once you are on your way towards getting to where you want to be, there are things you will want to consider in order to protect yourself in case anything unexpected happens. We will look at this in the next chapter.

Chapter 10
Future Planning

Mike Tyson, the former heavyweight boxing champion, famously once said "everybody has a plan until they get punched in the mouth". This is a thought that comes into my head quite regularly. (Perhaps that is something I should speak to my therapist about).

Although Iron Mike isn't someone well known for his deep philosophical thinking, I feel that this is actually an extremely shrewd observation. Life will constantly throw you curveballs.

Emergency Planning

We have already looked at the importance of putting some money away in the case of an emergency. While this can be difficult, it is good practice to aim to have at least three months' worth of your income set aside at any one time in order to tide you over in the event that you fall out of work or have some short-term financial issue.

How do I prepare for the unexpected?

Luckily, there are ways to protect yourself from suffering financial ruin in the event of an unexpected event. There are well established products that exist solely for the protection of wealth that allow you to carry on living your best life even if something comes along like a job loss or sickness.

The good news is that these products are generally cheaper the younger you start using them.

Unexpected redundancy, developing a critical illness or having to take an extended period off work due to mental illness or after an accident could throw you completely off track for your goals, especially if you do not have as much of an emergency fund set aside.

What are the chances?

Understanding the likelihood of having unfortunate events happen to you is very useful when planning ahead.

There are people called actuaries whose job it is to use maths and statistics to work out the likelihood of events happening to people in order to let companies manage risks and enable people to plan for these events if they ever take place.

To give you an example, according to recent calculations by the Institute and Faculty of Actuaries, an 18 year old non-smoker who plans to retire at state retirement age (68) has a 39% chance of having to take at least one month off work due to sickness at some stage before they reach retirement age.

An 18 year old non-smoker has a one in 5 chance of suffering a serious or critical illness that will stop them working at some point during their working career.

This same person on average has a 7% chance of dying before age 68.

Bad things happen in life but if you are prepared for them, they won't seem so bad

Have a play with a "what are my chances" calculator online and you might be surprised with just how likely you are to suffer an unfortunate event during your working life.

This is a good one that was put together by *Legal and General:*

https://www.legalandgeneral.com/adviser/protection/doing-business-with-us/tools-calculators/what-are-the-chances/

What if I get sick or critically ill?

The financial planning and insurance industries exist so that you can sleep better at night knowing that if anything were to happen to you (be it unemployment, illness or you have an accident), you can keep paying your bills until you can get back to work. If you are too ill to work again, if you've taken out a suitable policy you won't need to worry; all your needs will be taken care of for the rest of your days. As you get older and your responsibilities increase, you will want to ensure that if you get thrown one of these curve balls, it doesn't spell disaster.

"Fail to Prepare, Prepare to Fail."

I know that thinking about getting sick and dying isn't the cheeriest thing to be writing about, but it's important to be prepared. I've dealt with clients who have lost a husband/wife. They planned for the event that their partner might die and had cover in place. When the unfortunate death happened, they were able to ensure that their mortgage got paid off and their kids didn't have to move to a new school in a different area.

Sadly, I have also had clients that came to me after their partners had died and they hadn't planned for the event of this happening.

If there is no plan in place, things can get very difficult.

Not only do you have to deal with the emotional trauma, but you can face financial ruin on top of everything else. No one plans to die early, but it is important to make sure that if it happens, your loved ones are looked after.

You may have seen people with a cheesy motivational quote on social media that says, "Fail to Prepare, Prepare to Fail." Now, for the record I'm not a big "Live, Laugh, Love" type guy, but this little saying about the importance of planning is actually pretty wise.

Introducing Protection Products

I can't stress enough how important it is to have a plan in place in case things go wrong. Insurance products are often provided by banks, building societies and insurance companies.

It is very important to shop around and make sure that the product you have will actually be of benefit to you because each one will have a cost associated with it.

If you have an emergency fund set aside, then the cost of many types of insurance will be cheaper, as you will not need to make a claim for a longer period of time, making it less likely that you will need to actually use the product.

Car Insurance

If you want to drive a car legally in the UK, by law, you need to have car insurance.

The most basic form of cover makes sure that if something happens when you are on the road and you cause harm to someone else or damage their property, the insurance company will pay to put things right. You can pay a premium monthly or in one annual payment.

The more time you go without having to claim, the lower your premium will go. This is because the insurance companies don't like having to pay out money so if you can prove you are a good driver they will recognise that by giving you lower premiums.

Insurance for Younger People

A young person is more likely to crash a car than someone who is older and more experienced therefore they pay more. The good news, however, is that when it comes to insurance products that insure you against illness or death, the premiums will be cheaper the younger and healthier you are.

Protection Example

You have an affordable insurance policy in place that will pay you an income if anything happens to you. Let's say for example you take it out and keep it in place over ten years and you never have to use it. With most policies, when the term runs out, the policy ends, and you don't get any money back. When you first consider it, this might seem like wasted money.

If, however, you were to have a bad car crash and not have the policy in place, you might lose your job. This could lead to you having nowhere to live because you might struggle to pay your rent and medical expenses while you recover. This would have a massive negative impact on your finances and life in general. Without the policy in place, you could lose your home, fall into debt and suffer a really horrible time due to something completely outside your control.

Let's have a brief look at the most common insurance products

- **Car Insurance.** We've looked at this above and it is pretty straight forward. You pay a premium each month or each year, and while it remains in place your insurance company will step in and pay for any damage or harm you cause to anyone or anything else with your car (or your own car depending on the type of cover you have).
- **Income Protection.** This pays out an income if something happens that stops you working. (illness, injury or redundancy) You usually pay monthly and it will normally cover roughly 60% of your wage for a set period of time. The premium will be based on how long you want the payments to last and the amount of time you are happy to wait before the payments kick in.

- **Critical illness.** This is an insurance policy that you pay for monthly which is designed to pay out a tax free lump sum if you are diagnosed with a serious illness during the term of the policy. Each provider may have different illnesses that they cover so it is worth checking before taking one out.
- **Life Insurance.** There are lots of different forms of life insurance products, but the most commonly used ones will allow you to choose a term (a pre agreed length of time) and if you pass away, they will pay out a lump sum to take care of your loved ones. Most will pay out if you are diagnosed with a terminal illness and are given 12 months or less to live. The premium will be based on how much you want to leave, the length of the cover, your smoker status and your state of health.

A lot of people only get these when they purchase their first property however as I said before, it's very important to shop around as banks often just give you a life insurance quote with the mortgage that is much more expensive than it might be elsewhere and people don't ask any questions and end up paying through the nose.

What are the benefits of getting protection in place early?

Some people don't like the idea of paying for insurance because they think it might be too expensive.

As I said before, the great news in this chapter of non-stop depressing doom and gloom is that for a young person, if you are relatively healthy, insurance is much cheaper than it is for older people.

You also have the option of opting for a "guaranteed" non reviewable policy (i.e. one where the amount you pay isn't regularly reviewed) which could run for decades without increasing. It means you can get a low premium agreed based on your current state of health before any of the common health issues pop up later in life (diabetes, high blood pressure etc). Boom!

It will be cheaper if you don't smoke because smokers suffer so many more health problems than non-smokers. Another great reason why not to smoke if you needed one.

Writing a Will

As I've already said before, no one plans to die early. So, writing a will at a young age might seem unnecessary, but if you have ever heard stories of families arguing over a deceased relative's possessions, you'll know that it really can tear families apart.

For this reason, it's worth keeping in mind to get one written as early as possible and keep it up to date. You can contact a local solicitor who will help you do this.

Pension Planning

This might seem like the most boring thing you could ever talk about but like it or not, planning for your retirement is essential.

What is a Pension?

This is a way of saving for your retirement so that you can have some income when you stop working. You can do it through a workplace or privately or both. Your National Insurance contributions will go towards your state pension.

In times gone by, working people didn't really need to worry about pensions too much. They were set up so that if you worked for a company or had a government job (teacher, nurse etc) when you stopped working at 60 or 65, these plans would start paying out a generous income for life.

With people now living longer these schemes cost so much to run, the average pension today isn't as generous as it was for previous generations.

It is therefore going to be really important that young people today start saving towards their retirement as early as possible.

Auto Enrolment

It has recently become a legal requirement for employers to offer a pension scheme to their workers if you are over 22 and earn more than £10,000 a year.

The government is encouraging people to pay in as much as possible to reduce the strain on the public purse later on. The minimum amount you would contribute is 4% of your salary, the government tops this up by 1%, and then your employer has the responsibility of topping this up by a minimum of 3%.

State Pension

The state pension currently pays out roughly £750 a month for someone that qualifies for the full state pension (you currently need to have paid national insurance for 35 years by retirement to get this full amount). I do not want to be pessimistic, however with people living longer and all the debt that the government has built up after bailing out the banks in 2008, and then with Covid costing the economy so much on top of that, I would not be surprised if the State Pension rules look very different by the time you and I reach retirement age.

It keeps getting moved back later and later in life, and it is the most expensive type of benefit that the government has to pay out each year.

Additionally, the cost keeps getting bigger each year with people living longer than they used to.

With this in mind, I try to warn my clients to make their own private arrangements as well as contributing to the state pension and make sure they don't rely solely on the government to look after them in old age.

Pensions – The Ticking Time Bomb

Because pension schemes aren't as generous as they once were, and since people are living longer and not getting on the property ladder until later in life, many prominent voices have expressed concern that the average person in the UK will struggle in retirement and may even face poverty and stress... Not something you want to look forward to after a lifetime of hard work.

Research done by pension company Aegon in 2019 has predicted that even if someone were to get access to the full state pension and pay into an auto enrolment scheme from age 22, this would still leave them short by a considerable margin if they had been planning to live comfortably in retirement.

They have worked off average figures and the research is from a couple of years ago however it paints a pretty grim picture of the future many people will have unless they take action very early on.

Start Early and Worry Less

I can't stress enough just how important it is to start saving for retirement early and pay more than the minimum set out in basic workplace Auto Enrolment schemes if this is what you find yourself in.

When we looked at compound interest in the saving chapter, you will have seen just how quickly savings start to rack up once you start earning interest on interest - growth on growth.

Some bigger companies will offer more generous pensions, but for most of us, we will be offered the basic 8% total contribution.

Here are some of the eye-opening figures from the research conducted by Aegon:

"Someone who is auto enrolled into a workplace pension from age 22 might still face a gap of £106,500 in today's money. To plug that, they might need to pay in an extra 4% of earnings on top of the 5% they are currently required to pay under auto enrolment. But someone without any prior pensions auto enrolled at age 35 would need to pay an extra 13%."

Tax Relief

This is something that is very important to know about because by combining the powers of compounding and tax relief, you are much more likely to be able to save enough to be comfortable when you are old and grey.

HMRC allows savers to get a top up on pension contributions.

For an employed worker, every £80 you pay into a pension scheme as a basic rate (20%) taxpayer, you will get £100 in your pot. For higher rate taxpayers (40%) you can claim back even more. Higher rate taxpayers will be able to claim back 40% on all their contributions meaning that they get £100 for every £60 you save into a pension. If you are self-employed, you can use pension contributions to reduce your tax liability.

When do I want to retire?

Under current regulations someone who is in their 20s now will be able to access their private pension from age 57 (but this may change). This flexibility only came into effect in the last decade.

When it was first debated in 2014, Boris Johnson who was an MP at the time said "If people blow all their pensions on luxuries and end up living in a rusted Lamborghini eating dog food that is their look out"... Basically he was saying it's up to you the saver to be responsible how you spend your money.

The sad thing I note is that currently the average pension pot at retirement in the UK isn't enough to buy a new Lamborghini. Who says politicians are out of touch, eh?

The Importance of Becoming Financially Literate

By now I would hope you have learned some more about finance and are able to see why it is nothing to be afraid of. It can be fun learning more about managing your finances and rewarding when you set goals and then smash them. Money isn't everything, but it can make life so much easier if you become well informed and make wise choices early on. With all the current stresses that we've learned about in this guide, I believe that it is 100% essential you get your head around some of the basics we've covered here.

If it is something that doesn't come naturally to you or you can't get your head around at all, do not stress. There are people who you can turn to who can help you plan for a bright future. Financial advice from a trustworthy source can be sought out (www.unbiased.co.uk) and it is these people's sole purpose to create plans that are tailored to your needs and explain them to you so that you understand every bit of it.

Just remember to take advantage of free consultations, ensure you ask how much you would be charged if you took their advice, and always shop around.

Once you agree on a plan it is the adviser's responsibility to ensure you understand it so ask as many questions as you need to before you leave the office. (Trust me, I have these conversations with clients every day and I welcome these questions. I feel great when someone comes into the office without a clue and leaves happy with a better understanding of their options with a new plan in their mind).

You can find information on local advisers here:

https://www.moneyadviceservice.org.uk/en/articles/choosing-a-financial-adviser

An Exciting Lifelong Journey Ahead

The road to becoming financially healthy can be a long one. For some people it will come naturally but for others it will require more work and a little more support. I hated maths in school and my maths teacher will testify to the obscene number of times I got negative comments in my planner for my parents to sign. (Sorry Mr Gallagher. Sorry mammy.) Despite maths not being my favourite subject, I still went on to work in banking, then debt management and then financial planning. Eventually the numbers fall into place.

When you spend a bit of time to put a plan in place, then begin to see investments growing tax free, and you start ticking goals off your list, you will see how fulfilling and rewarding it is to take an interest in what happens to the money you earn each month.

Suggested Further Reading / Viewing

There are some great resources available online to help you on your journey towards financial health.

- I would recommend bookmarking the Money Charity's website to help you on your journey. They regularly update their site with useful resources, including webinars and money workshops: https://themoneycharity.org.uk/
- It is worth signing up for subscriptions with personal finance publications and keep your eye out for finance stories in the press. You can find one that matches your level of experience and follow it on social media. Additionally, once you start learning about investing, Investopedia can be a useful resource: https://www.investopedia.com/

- Before you start investing, if you would like to hear some information about the options available to you, there are a few people online who do a great job of explaining things in a way that is entertaining and easy to understand. A lot of them welcome questions and will interact with you if you drop comments below their videos.

  One such source I've found useful is a YouTube channel called *Damien Talks Money.* He's a nice guy who looks at investment options and gives his opinion on them and talks you through how the products work and the risks involved.

  Remember, this type of channel is for information purposes and are not recommendations specifically tailored for your circumstances. This guy does a great job of explaining money issues in a way that is funny and informative at the same time:

  Link to *Damien Talks Money's* Channel
  https://www.youtube.com/channel/UCjPR68IfHV0aY9s6cF5u0uQ

- MamaFurFur's Youtube channel: This is a channel run by a very clever lady from Scotland with all sorts of useful information on things like setting up side hustles, ways of getting out of debt, investing strategies and she even talks about the importance of mental health in some of her videos.

I highly recommend checking out some of her content. She covers the basics in straight forwards language and covers all sorts of more advanced things when you want to broaden your horizons. Start with the basics and work your way up!
https://www.youtube.com/channel/UCPvSN7kot8zJUreVzs-0y8A Search Mama Fur Fur on Youtube.

- I would recommend reading the book "*Rich Dad Poor Dad*" by Robert Kyosaki, available through Plata Publishing. This is a very popular book which I mentioned earlier in the guide that gives an interesting view on personal finance.
- Last but not least, *Coffeezilla* has a channel where he regularly uploads videos where he watches out for bad financial advice online, scam artists and warns his viewers. He observes trends and offers a platform for people to discuss issues within the finance industry. You can find him here:
https://www.youtube.com/channel/UCFQMnBA3CS502aghlcr0_aw or Search CoffeeZilla on Youtube.

Chapter 11

Final Thoughts

Hopefully, if you have managed to make it this far, this guide will have helped you develop a better understanding of real-world finance and set you on course to develop a healthy relationship with money.

I would hope you keep this book handy so that when these issues become relevant to your life, you can pick up the guide and it will be of some use. Some of the details (like tax rules and some of the products that are available) may change as time goes on, but hopefully there are enough links to good solid sources of information that will keep you up to date.

Using Your Newly Discovered Knowledge

Look out for friends and family members. Being kind to yourself is extremely important.

Equally, looking out for other members in the community, helping them succeed and live more happy, healthy lives will make you feel good too.

If you have learned something by reading this book that you think might be useful for other young people, suggest they have a look at some of the chapters that might help them, or you can simply give them a few pointers to help them on their way.

Make Learning A Habit

I hope this guide has been helpful, but keep in mind that the pursuit of knowledge should never end. I'm not suggesting that you should become a complete nerd reading the Financial Times every day! However, I truly believe that taking a bit of an interest in finance and keeping yourself up to date with what's happening in the world with regards to money and investing and keeping an eye on your goals regularly will hopefully set you up for a more successful and comfortable future.

I would like to take this opportunity to thank you for reading and wish you all the best on your journey towards financial health!

If you would like to contact me, get in touch via: fwfinancialhealth@gmail.com

Manufactured by Amazon.ca
Bolton, ON